HTML 3.2

Quick Reference, 2nd Edition

HTML 3.2

Quick Reference, 2nd Edition

Credits

President
Roland Elgey

Publisher
Stacy Hiquet

Publishing Manager
Fred Slone

Senior Title Manager
Bryan Gambrel

Editorial Services Director
Elizabeth Keaffaber

Managing Editor
Sandy Doell

Acquisitions Editor
Al Valvano

Production Editor
Sherri Fugit

Editor
Thomas Cirtin

Strategic Marketing Manager
Barry Pruett

Technical Editors
Jim O'Donnell
Dave Medinets

Product Marketing Manager
Kristine Ankney

Assistant Product Marketing Managers
Karen Hagen
Christy Miller

Technical Support Specialist
Nadeem Muhammed

Acquisitions Coordinator
Carmen Krikorian

Software Relations Coordinator
Susan D. Gallagher

Editorial Assistant
Andrea Duvall

Book and Cover Designer
Nathan Clement

Production Team
Maribeth Echard
Tim Neville
Kaylene Riemen
Donna Wright

Indexer
Tim Tate

Composed in *Frutiger* and *ITC Kabel* by Que Corporation.

We'd Like to Hear from You!

As part of our continuing effort to produce books of the highest possible quality, Que would like to hear your comments. To stay competitive, we really want you to let us know what you like or dislike most about this book or other Que products.

Please send your comments, ideas, and suggestions for improvement to:

The Expert User Team

Email: **euteam@que.mcp.com**

CompuServe: **72410,2077**

Fax: (317) 581-4663

Our mailing address is:

Expert User Team
Que Corporation
201 West 103rd Street
Indianapolis, IN 46290-1097

You may also visit our Team's home page on the World Wide Web:

http://www.mcp.com/que/developer_expert

Your comments will help us to continue publishing the best books available in today's market.

Thank you,

The Expert User Team

Contents at a Glance

Table of Contents

Contents

Contents

Contents

Contents

Contents

Contents

Contents

HTML 3.2 Quick Reference, 2nd Edition

Contents

Contents

Contents

INTRODUCTION

The explosive growth of the Internet has created a vast array of new programming languages and tools. There are new commands, new APIs, and new syntax structures to learn. Until now, there haven't been any comprehensive language or command references available for these new Internet tools. *HTML 3.2 Quick Reference*, *Second Edition* is the primary source programmers turn to for information and the one book they cannot do without.

Please remember this book is a quick reference. The definitions and text in the HTML Reference section are designed to *remind* you what the tags, attributes, and options are. If you need an introductory book, buy *HTML by Example* or *Special Edition Using HTML*, which are both published by Que.

You can also find extensive HTML references on the Internet. While writing this book, I made use of the HTML Reference Guide written by the Web Design Group at **http://www.htmlhelp.com**. You'll find the online guide to be well-written and logically organized.

So, you may ask yourself, "Why buy this book at all, if the material is available online?" That's a good question. This book is much easier to use than reading online pages, the Index is more extensive, and you don't have to wait for pages to download.

Using This Book

HTML 3.2 Quick Reference, *Second Edition* is designed to provide quick and easy access to commands, standards, and programming tips.

This book is not a tutorial; it's assumed that you already know the fundamentals of the various languages and standards. Instead, this book is a definitive reference work for the Web programmer.

There are five sections in this book: the Introduction, Quick Tables, HTML Reference Section, HTML Reference Tables, and the Glossary.

HTML 3.2 Quick Reference, 2nd Edition

The "Quick Tables" section provides a way to find specific HTML tags based on the task you need to perform.

The "HTML Reference Section" has an entry for every accepted (and entries anticipated to be accepted) tag in the various HTML standards and extensions in use. The entries are listed in alphabetical order.

Every effort has been made to build the most comprehensive and up-to-date reference of HTML in encyclopedic format. Note that there are several related conventions that are not part of the HTML standard but that can be called up or manipulated from an HTML document. Many of the most advanced math elements and server-side includes, for example, are not part of the HTML standards now in development. The scope of this book is focused on HTML standards observed by browsers offered by Netscape, Microsoft, and Mosaic and the HTML 2 and HTML 3.2 standards.

New tags will be added to subsequent editions of this book as they are recognized, adopted, and implemented in products such as Netscape Navigator, Internet Explorer, and Mosaic or as they're included in subsequent HTML standards.

Most HTML tags fall into families or functional categories. Tag categories are being developed by standards groups to foster tag enhancement efforts into clearly defined areas. The categories defined in this book coincide with the HTML 2 and HTML 3.2 specification categories with some minor modifications. The HTML 2 and HTML 3.2 specifications are thoroughly supported by Netscape and Microsoft. In addition, both companies have introduced their own enhancements in the form of tags called *extensions*.

HTML Tag Categories

Name	Description
General	General tags include the basic page formatting tags required in every HTML document.
Form	Form tags are used to accept input using plain HTML—as opposed to accepting input with ActiveX controls or Java applets.

Name	Description
Tables	Table tags are used to create row and column tables on your Web page. They are very useful to control how and where page elements are displayed. Some older browsers don't understand the Table tags, but they are so useful most Webmasters use them anyway.
Frame	Frame tags are used to partition the browser window into sections. Each section can have content that is independent from the others. Text-based Web browsers and some older graphical browsers can't understand the Frame tags. Therefore, creating a non-frame version of your Web site is generally a good idea.
Structural	Structural tags are used to represent the structure of a Web page. These tags organize the page into headers, paragraphs, and lists.
Miscellaneous	Miscellaneous tags are tags that don't fit into the other categories—of course, you already knew that... For example, some newer browsers use the <SCRIPT> tag to add JavaScript and VBScript elements to a page.
Entities	Entities are not really tags, but they are important. For example, you can use © in order to display a copyright on a Web page. You can find tables listing HTML entities in the "Miscellaneous Tables" section.
Backgrounds and Colors	Background and Color tags are used to control the background images and colors used in Web pages.
Lists	List tags are a subset of the Structural category. They let you create hierarchical lists and sublists in Web pages.
Dividers	Divider tags are used to visually separate areas of Web pages.
Links	Link tags are used to create the hyperlinks that HTML is famous for. When clicked, the browser loads the associated URL.
Graphics	Graphic tags control where and how an image is displayed.
Presentation	Presentation tags control how text is displayed. For example, you can display text as centered, bold, and italic.

The "HTML Reference Tables" section pulls together information that I've found very useful while editing Web pages. This section includes the HTML entities, a color table, and a list of UseNet newsgroups.

The "Glossary" section lists definitions for common words used with HTML.

No matter what you're looking for, make sure to make use of the Index in the back of the book. The Index arranges tags alphabetically, so you should be able to quickly locate your topic.

Other Helpful Que Books for Webmasters

Whether you're a beginning Webmaster or an old hand, Que has the best, most comprehensive set of books you can buy! Try any of the following books.

Beginner/Intermediate Level

- *HTML by Example*
- *Java by Example*
- *JavaScript by Example*
- *Perl 5 by Example*
- *VBScript by Example*

Intermediate/Expert Level

- *Special Edition Using ActiveX*
- *Special Edition Using CGI*
- *Special Edition Using HTML* and *Platinum Edition, Using HTML 3.2*
- *Special Edition Using Java* and *Platinum Edition, Using Java 1.1*
- *Special Edition Using Perl for Web Programming*
- *Special Edition Using VBScript*

Quick References

- *Java Quick Reference*
- *JavaScript Quick Reference*

Don't forget to check Que's Web site at **http://www.quecorp.com** for updates on subsequent releases of this book and other HTML references from Que.

Conventions Used in This Book

Que has over a decade of experience writing and developing the most successful computer books available. With that experience, we've learned what special features help readers the most. Look for these special features throughout the book to enhance your learning experience.

Several font conventions are used in this book to help make reading, referencing, and finding things easier. They are the following:

- *Italic type* is used to emphasize the author's points or to introduce new terms.
- Screen messages, code listings, and command samples appear in monospace typeface.
- Anything you are asked to type appears in **boldface**.

TIP Tips present short advice on a quick or often overlooked procedure. These include shortcuts that can save you time.

NOTE A note provides additional information that may help you avoid problems, or offers advice that relates to the topic.

CAUTION Cautions warn you about potential problems that a procedure may cause, unexpected results, and mistakes to avoid.

Longer discussions not integral to the flow of the chapter are set aside as sidebars. Look for these sidebars to find out even more information.

About the "HTML Reference" Section

The "HTML Reference" section is the part of this book that describes HTML tags and attributes. Some tags occupy more than a single page so that they are documented properly.

The following sections describe the kind of information you can expect to find on each page in the "HTML Reference" section.

Command Header

This section displays the name of the HTML element described on that page or pages.

Compliance

This section explores compliance issues and the relevance to the content of the reference section. The following icons are used to indicate whether the reader can expect a given element to work properly if he or she is staying within the scope of these levels of compliance:

Netscape

This icon indicates that the latest versions of Netscape Navigator will render this element properly.

Internet Explorer

This icon indicates that the latest versions of Internet Explorer will render this element properly.

Mosaic/XMosaic

This icon indicates that the latest versions of Mosaic and XMosaic will render this element properly.

HTML 2

This icon indicates compliance with this set of standards.

HTML 3.2

This icon indicates compliance with this set of standards.

Syntax

This section provides an example of how the covered element appears in an HTML document. It includes beginning and ending tags if both are used.

Definition

This section defines the use for the element as originally intended. Any general discussion of the element appears in this section.

Example Syntax

This section provides an example of how the element is used in an actual line in an HTML document. Also, if a figure is displayed on the same page, every effort has been made to display the result of the "Example Syntax" in that figure.

In Actual Use

If a figure (screen shot and caption) imparts value in a visual way, it is included here. The "Example Syntax" is used for this illustration. If a figure isn't useful, the "In Actual Use" section is not included.

Related Elements

If appropriate to the element being discussed, this section has a table that informs the reader of related HTML elements that can be used outside or inside the discussed element. Some elements do not require a "Related Elements" table.

HTML QUICK TABLES

Research has shown that people use reference materials in two ways. People who already have basic knowledge of concepts can recognize keywords in a book's Index and find what they need. People who don't necessarily know what to look for in the Index often rely on the Table of Contents to find information on a more topical footing.

To support these two different mindsets, we've produced two Quick Tables that speed you to several other tables containing specific page numbers for the information you seek. These tables act as agents to lead you to the information you seek. Less guesswork, less hassle, and less time wasted!

How to Use Quick Tables

The "Building Pages Task-by-Task" Table leads you to the most popular HTML tags used when authoring Web page elements.

The "Top Commands in Each Category" Table directs you to other tables where the most popular tags and attributes are listed by the most popular categories. Many people discover that moving between tables (and the elements that they point to) can help find a tag or attribute in a minimum amount of time!

Building Pages Task-by-Task

To find new ways to work with various HTML tags and their attributes, refer to the jump table on this page. Find a category that interests you and jump to a corresponding table that can help you completely understand these basic concepts. Then use your new-found knowledge to build your Web pages.

Building Pages Task-by-Task

Format Your Text

The tags listed on this page are used to change the appearance of text on a Web page. Managing the choice, color, and emphasis of text is a key factor in making your pages easier to read and memorable to the reader.

Tags	Description	Go to Page...
`<B>`	Bold	26
`<BASEFONT>`	Sets default font attributes	30
`<BIG>`	Increments font size by one	33
`<BLINK>`	Makes text blink	34
`<CODE>`	Fixed-width font	44
`<EM>`	Emphasized text	58
`<FONT>`	Sets font attributes	61
`<I>`	Italic	84
`<KBD>`	Fixed-width font	93
`<PRE>`	Fixed-width font	126
`<S>`	Strikethrough	131

Tags	Description	Go to Page...
`<SAMP>`	Smaller fixed-width font	131
`<SMALL>`	Decrements font size by one	139
`<STRIKE>`	Strikethrough	143
`<STRONG>`	Emphasized text	143
`<SUB>`	Subscript text	145
`<SUP>`	Superscript text	145
`<TT>`	Fixed-width text	157
`<U>`	Underline	158
`<VAR>`	Smaller fixed-width font	161

Structure Your Text

The HTML tags in this table represent the HTML tags used for organizing text on an HTML page. A good HTML author thinks about the way text is ordered and placed on Web pages. Use these tags to structure your text so that readers can easily and quickly understand the meaning.

Tags	Description	Go to Page...
`<ADDRESS>`	Address information	21
`<AU>`	Author information	26
`<BLOCKQUOTE>`	Indents a block of text	34
`<BQ>`	Indents a block of text	37
` `	Line break	38
`<CENTER>`	Centers text	42
`<CITE>`	Citation information	43
`<CODE>`	Computer language statements	44
`<CREDIT>`	Names blockquote or figure source	52

Tags	Description	Go to Page...
<DIR>	Narrow compact list	54
<H1> to <H6>	Specifies header level	69
<HR>	Horizontal rule	78
<KBD>	Input from a keyboard	93
<LANG>	Changes language	94
<MENU>	List of Items	105
<NOTE>	Note, Caution, or Warning	121
<OL>	Numbered list	122
<P>	Paragraph	124
<PERSON>	Name of an individual	126
<PLAINTEXT>	Ignores HTML tags	126
<PRE>	Preformatted text	126
<TABLE>	Table of information	146
<TITLE>	Title of the Web page	155
<CODE>	Computer language statements	44

Display a Graphic Image

The tags listed in this table are used for displaying graphical images on a Web page. The <BODY> tag controls the background image while the <IMG> tag controls the foreground images.

Tags	Description	Go to Page...
<BODY BACKGROUND= "graphic file">	Background image	27
<IMG>	Image	86

Presenting a Background

These tags play a role in controlling the background of a Web page. While they are few in number, the sensible use of background imagery and audio has a profound impact on any Web page.

Tags	Description	Go to Page...
`<BODY BACKGROUND= "graphic file">`	Background image	27
`<BODY BGCOLOR= "color">`	Background color	31
`<BODY BGPROPERTIES= "fixed">`	Watermark image	32
`<BGSOUND>`	Background sound	32

Top Commands in Each Category

This table directs you to the most commonly used tags in the most popular tag categories. This table is especially useful to those who normally rely on the detailed Index found at the end of this and other reference books.

Top Commands in Each Category

To Find the Top Commands for...	Go to Page...
Colors	31
Forms	63
Frames	65
Lists	94
Tables	146

Colors

The colors used on your Web pages can determine the contrast and hence legibility of your Web page. Use the tags and attributes in this table to change the colors of your backgrounds, text, tables, and so on.

Tags and Attributes	Description	Go to Page...
`<BODY ALINK= "color">`	Active hyperlink color	22
`BGCOLOR` (attribute)	Background color	31
`<FONT COLOR= "color">`	Font color	61
`<BODY LINK= "color">`	Link color	96
`<BODY VLINK= "color">`	Visited hyperlink color	162

Forms

Forms give the HTML author a way to collect information for processing or forwarding. They are mainly used in conjunction with CGI programs or scripts on a Web server. The tags in this table are used to present the elements of a form on an HTML page.

Tags	Description	Go to Page...
`<FORM>`	Creates a form	63
`<INPUT>`	Simple input field	88
`<SELECT>`	Listbox input field	134
`<TEXTAREA>`	Multiline input field	151

Frames

Frames are another way that you can create a unique interface for your Web site. Frames are ideal for tables of contents, fixed interface elements, better forms, and results.

Tags	Description	Go to Page...
`<FRAME>`	Creates a frame	65
`<FRAMESET>`	Replaces <BODY>	66
`<NOFRAMES>`	For non-frame browsers	118

Lists

Organizing thoughts and short sentences into meaningful, easy-to-read lists makes your pages easier to comprehend and more user-friendly. The tags in this table are used to present text in different list formats.

Tags	Description	Go to Page...
`<DIR>`	Narrow compact list	54
`<DL>`	Definition list	55
`<MENU>`	Compact list	105
`<OL>`	Ordered list	122
`<UL>`	Bulleted list	159

Tables

Tables are a recent but welcome addition to HTML authoring. Tables help you organize text and graphics so they relate to each other in rows and columns for easier reading.

Tags	Description	Go to Page...
`<CAPTION>`	Table caption	39
`<TABLE>`	Creates a table	146
`<TD>`	Table cell	149
`<TH>`	Table header	153
`<TR>`	Table row	156

HTML REFERENCE SECTION

In this HTML Reference section, you'll find an entry for every accepted element or *tag* (and those anticipated to be accepted) for the various HTML standards and extensions in use. There are also entries for all of the major tag *attributes*. A tag attribute modifies the effect of a tag or provides information needed by the Web browser. For example, you can use the `<COLOR>` and `<SIZE>` attributes with the `<FONT>` tag.

The elements in this section are in alphabetical order, as you would expect to find in a dictionary. If a tag manipulates the visual presentation of a browser, a figure is provided to help illustrate the effect created by the use of that tag.

Every effort has been made to build the most comprehensive and up-to-date reference of the Hypertext Markup Language. There are several related conventions that are not part of the HTML standard, but can be called up or manipulated from an HTML document. For example, ActiveX and Server-Side Includes are not part of the HTML standards; therefore, they are outside the scope of this book.

NOTE For more information on ActiveX, check out Que's *Special Edition Using ActiveX.*

The entries in this reference section contain the following information (see Table 2.1):

Table 2.1 Types of Information Included for Each HTML Element

Information Type	Description
Heading	The name of the HTML element.
Compliance	Icons indicate which standard supports the element: Netscape, Internet Explorer, Mosaic/XMosaic, HTML 2, and/or HTML 3.2.

continues

Table 2.1   Continued

Information Type	Description
Syntax	The syntax of the element.
Definition	A general discussion of the element.
Example Syntax	An example of the element as it might appear in HTML.
Figure	Some elements have a figure associated with them.
Related Elements	Some elements have related elements; if so, you'll find them here.

The rest of this section is devoted to the HTML elements.

!--

Compliance

Syntax

`<!--...-->`

Definition

The `<comment>` tag lets you place comments in the code that can be seen only while editing. Web browsers simply ignore any text inside this tag. Commenting your HTML code is important when the newer, complicated tags are used.

Category

None

Example Syntax

```
<!-- Document: INDEX.HTM Version: 1.6 Date:1996/03/
25 17:33:48 -->
```

A

Compliance

Syntax

```
<A HREF="url" NAME="anchor">...</A>
```

Definition

The anchor tag denotes a hypertext link. Nearly any HTML element can be placed inside the `<A>` tag except another `<A>` tag. The `<A>` tag has the following attributes:

- HREF - The `HREF` attribute specifies where the browser goes when the link is clicked. You can use any valid URL as the target, including http://, news:, gopher://, mailto:, nntp://, telnet://, and wais://. For example, both HREF=**"http://www.codebits.com"** and HREF=**"mailto:medined@planet.net"** are valid.

- NAME - The `NAME` attribute indicates that the elements inside the `<A>` tag can be a target for an HREF. In other words, the `NAME` attribute creates an intra-page anchor. If you have `<A NAME="Testing"><H2>Testing</H2></A>` in a file called bar.html, then you can jump directly to that `H2` heading using `<A HREF="bar.html#Testing">Link to Testing Section</A>`.

Category

Links

Example Syntax

```
<A NAME="First Heading"><H1>First Heading</H1></A>
<P>This is a paragraph.</P>
<A NAME="Second Heading"><H1>Second Heading</H1></
A>
<P>This is another paragraph. Click <A HREF="#First
Heading">here</A>
to return to the first heading.</P>
```

The "here" text under the second heading is a hyperlink back to the first heading. The pound sign is used to reference NAME targets inside Web pages. URLs refer to the whole Web page and NAMEs refer to the anchors indicated by the <A> tag.

ABBREV

Syntax

```
<ABBREV>...</ABBREV>
```

Definition

The proposed abbreviation tag changes the contents to logically represent abbreviations. It is not currently implemented in any browsers known of at this time.

ACRONYM

Syntax

```
<ACRONYM>...</ACRONYM>
```

Definition

The proposed <acronym> tag changes the contents to logically represent acronyms. It is not currently implemented in any browsers known of at this time.

ADDRESS

Compliance

Syntax

```
<ADDRESS >...</ADDRESS>
```

Definition

The `<address>` tag is used to indicate that a body of text is an address. A good use for this tag might be as a standard element in your Web pages to indicate the point of contact in an organization or company. You can use most <HTML> tags inside the address tag to format the display of the text. Normally, the text will be displayed in italic and might be indented.

Category

Structural

Example Syntax

```
<ADDRESS>
 Robert Mullen
 <BR>Box 32<BR>
 <BR>Chicago Park, CA 95712-0032
</ADDRESS>
```

ALIGN (attribute)

Compliance

Syntax

`<tag ALIGN="alignment">`

Definition

The ALIGN attribute applies formatting to a body of text using LEFT, RIGHT, JUSTIFY, CENTER, or TEXTTOP) or a graphic using TOP, MIDDLE, or BOTTOM.

Related Elements

The ALIGN attribute is used by the APPLET, CAPTION, DIV, H1, H2, H3, H4, H5, H6, HR, IMG, INPUT, MARQUEE, P, TABLE, TD, TEXTAREA, TH, and TR.

Example Syntax

`<IMG SRC="MYFILE.GIF" ALIGN=TOP>`

ALINK (attribute)

Compliance

Syntax

`<BODY ALINK=color>`

Definition

The ALINK attribute defines the color of the active link. There can be only one active link—the one currently being selected.

Related Elements

The ALINK attribute is used by the `<BODY>` tag.

Example Syntax

`<BODY ALINK="Red" LINK="Blue" VLINK="Black">`

APP

The ⟨APP⟩ tag has been replaced by the ⟨APPLET⟩ tag.

APPLET

Compliance

 3 | 3.2

Syntax

```
<APPLET ALIGN="alignment" ALT="alternate text"
    CODE="java class" CODEBASE="url"
    HEIGHT="numPixels" HSPACE="numPixels"
    NAME="appletName" VSPACE="numPixels"
    WIDTH="numPixels">...</APPLET>
```

Definition

The ⟨APPLET⟩ tag identifies and invokes a Java applet. The use of Java applets is beyond the scope of this book (see *Java by Example,* another Que book, for more information). Web browsers that don't understand Java will display the content between the ⟨APPLET⟩...⟨/APPLET⟩ pair. Briefly, the attributes of the ⟨APPLET⟩ tag are:

- ALIGN - The display placement for the applet.
- ALT - The text that is displayed when the Java application can't or isn't allowed to run.
- CODE - The name of the applet's class file.
- CODEBASE - The URL of the applet's class file.
- HEIGHT - The height of the applet's display window.
- HSPACE - The amount of reserved space at the sides of the applet.
- NAME - The applet's name is used for intra-applet communications.

- VSPACE - The amount of reserved space at the top and bottom of the applet.
- WIDTH - The width of the applet's display window.

Category

None

Related Elements

The <PARAM> tag is used to pass information to applets. The information can be used to initialize internal applet variables and change the behavior of the applet.

AREA

Compliance

Syntax

<AREA ALT="*alternate text*" COORDS="*coordinates*"
  HREF="*url*" NOHREF SHAPE="*shape*">

Definition

The <AREA> tag specifies an area of an image. If the image is clicked in the area specified by the coordinates, then the Web browser loads the URL specified in the <AREA> tag. The attributes of the <AREA> tag are

- ALT - The text displayed by browsers that don't understand the AREA tag.
- COORDS - The coordinates of a series of points, defined as x, y pixel locations, where (0, 0) is the upper-left corner. When SHAPE=rect, the coordinates are "left, top, right, bottom." When SHAPE=circle, the coordinates are "center_x, center_y, radius." When SHAPE=poly, the coordinates are successive x, y vertices of the polygon.

- HREF - The URL that is loaded when the user clicked in the region defined by the <AREA> tag.
- NOHREF - The NOHREF attribute indicates that no links should be generated by this area.
- SHAPE - The shape of the area. Valid values are RECT, CIRCLE, POLY, and DEFAULT. The default shape covers the whole image map and is used to provide a default hyperlink.

Example Syntax

You can see the following example in action at **http://www.purplecanyon.com**. Notice that comments are intelligently used to document the <MAP> tag.

```
<MAP NAME="menu">
 <!-- #$AUTHOR:Purple Canyon Web Designs -->
 <!-- #$DATE:Mon Jan 06 05:55:25 1997 -->
 <!-- #$PATH:C:\web projects\Web
Projects\purplecanyon\images\ -->
 <!-- #$GIF:rocks_h.jpg -->
 <AREA SHAPE=CIRCLE COORDS="63,48,49"
HREF="graphix.html">
 <AREA SHAPE=CIRCLE COORDS="133,126,48"
HREF="why.html">
 <AREA SHAPE=CIRCLE COORDS="228,105,44"
HREF="clients.html">
 <AREA SHAPE=RECT COORDS="134,182,239,249"
HREF="prices.html">
 <AREA SHAPE=POLY
COORDS="10,148,23,227,111,203,45,123,10,148"
   HREF="contact.html">
 <AREA SHAPE=default HREF="http://
www.purplecanyon.com">
</MAP>
<img src="images/rocks_h.jpg" width=265 height=261
  border=0 alt="Choose!!!!!" usemap=#menu>
```

Related Elements

The <AREA> tag is only allowed inside of <MAP> tags. In addition, <MAP> tags are useless without a related <IMG USEMAP=" *map name*"> tag.

AU

Compliance

Syntax

`<AU>...</AU>`

Definition

The `<AU>` tag is used to identify the authors of an HTML document. This tag is most commonly used by groups of HTML authors working in a cooperative environment. The `<AU>` tag often appears in corporate and commercially prepared Web pages.

Category

Miscellaneous

Example Syntax

`<AU>Authors: Harold and Tim Robbins. Copyright 1996.</AU>`

B

Compliance

Syntax

`<B>...</B>`

Definition

The $\langle B \rangle$ tag displays text in **bold**. You might also consider using the $\langle BIG \rangle$, $\langle EM \rangle$, or $\langle STRONG \rangle$ tags instead of $\langle B \rangle$. The $\langle B \rangle$ tag can be used inside nearly every other tag. The opposite is also true. Nearly every other tag can be used inside the $\langle B \rangle \ldots \langle /B \rangle$ tag pair.

Category

Presentation

Example Syntax

```
Be the <B>first</B> person to own this
<B>amazing</B> product!
```

BACKGROUND (attribute)

Compliance

Example Syntax

```
<BODY BACKGROUND="url of graphic file">

<TABLE ALIGN="alignment" BACKGROUND="url of graphic
file"
    BGCOLOR="color" BORDER="numPixels"
    BORDERDARK="color" BORDERLIGHT="color"
    CELLPADDING="numPixels" CELLSPACING="numPixels"
    WIDTH="values">...</TABLE>
```

Definition

The BACKGROUND attribute specifies a graphics file to be tiled behind all other text and graphics on a page or table. Only Internet Explorer supports the BACKGROUND attribute for the $\langle TABLE \rangle$ tag (see Figure 2.1).

Category

Backgrounds

Example Syntax

<BODY BACKGROUND="hirs.jpg">

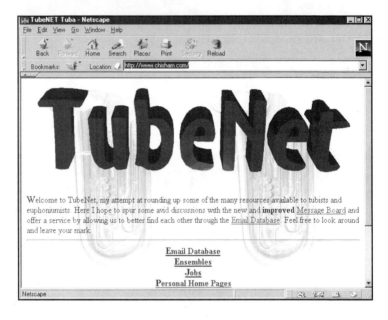

Fig. 2.1   This is an application of the BACKGROUND attribute.

BANNER

I believe the <BANNER> tag has been superseded by the <FRAME> tag. The <BANNER> tag was a proposed tag that would let you define corporate logos, navigation aids, and other information that shouldn't be scrolled.

BASE

Compliance

Syntax

`<BASE HREF="url" TARGET="target">`

Definition

The `<BASE>` tag specifies the base URL (the `HREF` attribute) for all other HREFs used in the document, allowing absolute URLs to be specified as relative ones within the document. This allows the document and its components to be moved easily (only the `<BASE>` tag needs to be changed, not all of the URLs). The `TARGET` attribute defines a default target window for all hyperlinks.

Category

Links

Example Syntax

`<BASE HREF="http://www.askamerica.com/index.htm" TARGET="middle">`

Related Elements

The `<BASE>` tag is only allowed within the `<HEAD>` tag. Both the `HREF` and `TARGET` attributes have their own definitions.

BASEFONT

Compliance

Syntax

```
<BASEFONT SIZE=size>
```

Definition

The `<BASEFONT>` tag lets you set the default font size for the Web page. The `SIZE` attribute can be valued from 1 through 7. These numbers do not map directly to specific font sizes. Instead, the Web browser has a set of preferences which includes the default display font. The default display font is associated with a `SIZE` of 3.

If you reduce the `SIZE` to 2, then the actual display font used will be larger than the default display font. If you increase the `SIZE` to 4, then the actual display font will be smaller than the default display font.

Category

Presentation

Example Syntax

```
<BASEFONT SIZE=4>
```

Related Elements

You can also affect the display font size by using the `<BIG>`, `<FONT>`, and `<SMALL>` tags.

BGCOLOR (attribute)

Compliance

Syntax

```
<BODY BGCOLOR=color>

<MARQUEE ALIGN="alignment" BEHAVIOR="options"
    BGCOLOR="color" DIRECTION="direction"
    HEIGHT="numPixels" HSPACE="numPixels"
    LOOP="options" SCROLLAMOUNT="numPixels"
    SCROLLDELAY="numMilliseconds"
    VSPACE="numPixels"
    WIDTH="numPixels">...</MARQUEE>
```

Definition

The BGCOLOR attribute controls the background color of the page. You can either use text-based color names, such as RED, GREEN, or BLUE, or you can specify colors as hexadecimal numbers. The list of color names is located in the "Miscellaneous Tables" section of this book.

Category

Backgrounds, Colors

Example Syntax

```
<BODY BGCOLOR="RED">
```

or

```
<BODY BGCOLOR=#ff0000>
```

BGPROPERTIES (attribute)

Compliance

Syntax

```
<BODY BACKGROUND=" graphic file"
BGPROPERTIES="FIXED" >
```

Definition

The BGPROPERTIES attribute uses a single copy of the background image in the background of the page instead of tiling the background images repeatedly (see the example of the cloud image for the BACK-GROUND attribute). This creates an impression much like that of a watermark seen on traditional stationery.

Category

Backgrounds

Example Syntax

```
<BODY BACKGROUND="logo.gif" BGPROPERTIES="FIXED">
```

BGSOUND

Compliance

Syntax

```
<BGSOUND SRC=" url of sound file" LOOP=" numSeconds">
```

Definition

The `<BGSOUND>` tag plays a background sound file (WAV, AU, or MIDI) when a viewer with sound capability visits the page. The sound file plays when the document is loaded by the browser. The `SRC` attribute indicates the location of the source file. The `LOOP` attribute determines the number of times the audio file is played. For example, a `LOOP` value of 4 plays the sound four times and a `LOOP` value of `INFINITE` plays the sound repeatedly.

NOTE Mosaic will not play a MIDI file using the `<BGSOUND>` tag.

Category

Miscellaneous

Example Syntax

```
<BGSOUND SRC="laughter.wav" LOOP=INFINITE>
```

BIG

Compliance

Syntax

```
<BIG>...</BIG>
```

Definition

The `<BIG>` tag increases the font size of text by one size. For example, you may want to emphasize words in a sentence by making them one font size larger.

Category

Presentation

Example Syntax

```
<P><BIG>Big</BIG> is beautiful!</P>
```

BLINK

Compliance

Syntax

```
<BLINK>...</BLINK>
```

Definition

The `<BLINK>` tag directs the browser to blink the specified text. Only Netscape supports this tag. You should not use the `<BLINK>` tag with more than one or two words of text. Otherwise, the reader will be forced to wait for the text to reappear before being able to continue reading.

Category

Presentation

Example Syntax

```
<BLINK>Click a button!</BLINK>
```

BLOCKQUOTE

Compliance

Syntax

```
<BLOCKQUOTE>...</BLOCKQUOTE>
```

Definition

The `<BLOCKQUOTE>` tag indents its contents on both sides and acts like a `<P>` tag by adding paragraph breaks (whitespace) both above and below the content. Some browsers also display the contents in italics, but not Netscape or Internet Explorer. If you want italicized text, use the `<I>` tag.

Because this is a structural element, there are many tags that don't logically belong between the `<BLOCKQUOTE>...</BLOCKQUOTE>` pair. For example, forms, headers, and tables don't belong inside a quote. On the other hand, it is perfectly acceptable to use any of the presentation tags and even the list tags.

Category

Structural

Example Syntax

```
<BLOCKQUOTE>"in the future, everybody will be
famous ..." <AU>Andy Warhol</AU>.</BLOCKQUOTE>
```

BODY

Compliance

Syntax

```
<BODY BACKGROUND=" url of graphic file "
   BGPROPERTIES="fixed"
   TEXT=" color"
   LINK=" color" ALINK=" color" VLINK=" color">...</
BODY>
```

Definition

All of the *content* in a Web page occurs inside the `<BODY>` tag. The `<BODY>` tag has the following attributes:

- BACKGROUND - The `BACKGROUND` attribute controls the background image used for the Web page.
- BGPROPERTIES - The `BGPROPERTIES` attribute determines if the background image is tiled or not tiled. However, the `BGPROPERTIES` attribute does seem to be supported yet.
- TEXT - The `TEXT` attribute controls the color of the page's text.
- LINK - The `LINK` attribute controls the color of the non-visited hyperlinked text on the page.
- ALINK - The `ALINK` attribute controls the color of the active hyperlinked text on the page. There can be only one active link— the one currently being selected.
- VLINK - The `VLINK` attribute controls the color of the visited hyperlinked text on the page.

Category

Structural

Example Syntax

```
<HTML>
 <HEAD>
  <TITLE>Using the BODY Tag</TITLE>
 </HEAD>
 <BODY>
  <H1>Heading One</H1>
  <P>Paragraph One</P>
 </BODY>
</HTML>
```

Related Elements

Information *about* the Web is located inside the `<HEAD>` tag. You can find out how to specify colors in the entry for the `COLOR` attribute.

BORDER (attribute)

Compliance

Syntax

```
<IMG BORDER="width in pixels" SRC="url of graphic
file">

<TABLE ALIGN="alignment" BORDER="width in pixels">
```

Definition

The BORDER attribute controls the border displayed around a table or an image. Images inside the <A> tag are usually displayed with a border to indicate the clickable area. You can prevent the border from being displayed by using a BORDER value of zero.

Category

None

Example Syntax

```
<A HREF="http://www.netscape.com">
 <IMG ALT="[Netscape Icon]" BORDER=5
SRC="netscape.gif">
</A>
```

BQ (obsolete)

The <BQ> tag was proposed as an enhancement or replacement for the <BLOCKQUOTE> tag. However, it was never used.

BR

Compliance

Syntax

```
<BR CLEAR="options">
```

Definition

The `<BR>` tag inserts a line break in an HTML document. The `CLEAR` attribute (LEFT, RIGHT, ALL, or NONE) is used to control text wrapping around the image when using `ALIGN` attribute of the `<IMG>` tag. When `ALIGN` is LEFT, you can force the wrapping text to drop directly to the bottom of the image by using a `CLEAR` attribute with a value of LEFT. Similarly, you can avoid text wrapping with a right-aligned image by using a `CLEAR` attribute with a value of RIGHT.

Category

Presentation

Example Syntax

```
<!-- Using line breaks inside a paragraph tag -->
<P>Hi. Thanks for writing. My address is
<BR>24 West High Street
<BR>New York City, NY 11121</P>
```

NOTE I find that placing the `<BR>` at the left margin of my HTML code makes the code easier to understand. Frequently, long HTML code lines stretch past the right edge of my editor window. Therefore, placing the `<BR>` tag in the right margin means continual skipping to the end of a line in order to check for line breaks.

Related Elements

The `ALIGN` attribute is described further in its own entry.

CAPTION

Compliance

Syntax

```
<CAPTION ALIGN="alignment">...</CAPTION>
```

Definition

The `<CAPTION>` tag places a header or caption directly before the rows and columns of a table and therefore must be included within a `<TABLE>` tag. The `ALIGN` attribute is used in two ways. You can place the caption at the top or bottom of the table by setting `ALIGN` to TOP or BOTTOM. You can also control the horizontal placement of the caption. An `ALIGN` attribute with a value of LEFT moves the caption to the left-hand margin. An `ALIGN` attribute with a value of RIGHT moves the caption to the right-hand margin. If no horizontal alignment is given, the caption is centered.

Category

Tables

Example Syntax

```
<TABLE>
 <CAPTION>Captions are centered by default
</CAPTION>
</TABLE>
```

CELLPADDING (attribute)

Compliance

Syntax

```
<TABLE ALIGN="alignment" BGCOLOR="color"
BORDER="numPixels"
    BORDERDARK="color" BORDERLIGHT="color"
    CELLPADDING="numPixels" CELLSPACING="numPixels"
    WIDTH="values">...</TABLE>
```

Definition

The CELLPADDING attribute of the <TABLE> tag controls the amount of extra space around a cell's contents. If the CELLPADDING is zero, cell content is only one pixel away from the cell border. I find most tables are more esthetic when CELLPADDING is five pixels.

Category

Tables

Example Syntax

```
<TABLE BORDER=5 CELLPADDING=5 CELLSPACING=0>
 <TR BGCOLOR="Gray">
  <TD ALIGN="Center">1</TD>
  <TD>Oakwood Manor</TD>
 </TR>
 <TR BGCOLOR="Silver" >
  <TD ALIGN="Center">2</TD>
  <TD>Greystoke Woods</TD>
 </TR>
 <TR BGCOLOR="Gray">
  <TD ALIGN="Center">3</TD>
  <TD>Turing Laurel</TD>
 </TR>
</TABLE>
```

CELLSPACING (attribute)

Compliance

Syntax

```
<TABLE ALIGN=" alignment" BGCOLOR=" color"
BORDER=" numPixels"
    BORDERDARK=" color" BORDERLIGHT=" color"
    CELLPADDING=" numPixels" CELLSPACING=" numPixels"
    WIDTH=" values">...</TABLE>
```

Definition

The CELLSPACING attribute of the <TABLE> tag controls the width of cell borders displayed in tables.

Category

Table

Example Syntax

```
<TABLE BORDER=5 CELLPADDING=5  CELLSPACING=10>
 <TR BGCOLOR="Gray">
  <TD ALIGN="Center">1</TD>
  <TD>Oakwood Manor</TD>
 </TR>
 <TR BGCOLOR="Silver" >
  <TD ALIGN="Center">2</TD>
  <TD>Greystoke Woods</TD>
 </TR>
 <TR BGCOLOR="Gray">
  <TD ALIGN="Center">3</TD>
  <TD>Turing Laurel</TD>
 </TR>
</TABLE>
```

CENTER

Compliance

Syntax

```
<CENTER>...</CENTER>
```

Definition

The `<CENTER>` tag centers its contents. Centered text can be very effective to display short, narrow lists. You should try to avoid creating paragraphs of centered text because the reader will find the jagged left margin hard to follow.

Category

Structural

Example Syntax

```
<CENTER>
 <P>This is a centered paragraph</P>
 <IMG SRC="logo.gif" ALT="centered image">
</CENTER>
```

CHECKED (attribute)

Compliance

Syntax

```
<INPUT TYPE="type" CHECKED>
```

Definition

The CHECKED attribute sets the value of a check box or option input field to checked or on. If the CHECKED attribute is not present in the <INPUT> tag, that particular input field does not have a checked value.

Category

Forms

Example Syntax

```
<FORM>
 Please select a vegetable:
 <BR><INPUT TYPE="checkbox" NAME="vegetable"
VALUE="Brocolli" CHECKED> Brocolli
 <BR><INPUT TYPE="checkbox" NAME="vegetable"
VALUE="Spinach"> Spinach
</FORM>
```

CITE

Compliance

Syntax

```
<CITE>...</CITE>
```

Definition

The <CITE> tag is used to represent a citation. Browsers display the content with an italic font. Citation should only be used to identify the titles of cited works.

Category

Structural

Example Syntax

```
<CITE>Shame of Man</CITE> by <AU>Piers Anthony</AU>
is both compelling and thought-provoking.
```

CODE

Compliance

Syntax

```
<CODE>...</CODE>
```

Definition

The <CODE> tag is used to represent small computer language frag-ments—typically inside paragraph text. Multiline language listings should use the <PRE> tag. The contents of the <CODE> tag usually appear in a fixed-width font.

Category

Structural

Example Syntax

```
<P>When assigning a value to a variable use the =
sign. For example, <CODE>$variable = 10;</CODE>.
```

COL (not used)

The little implemented `<COL>` tag was proposed to modify the display of tables. It was supposed to specify default values (alignment, width, and so on) for table columns.

COLGROUP (not used)

The little implemented `<COLGROUP>` tag was proposed to group table columns and specify the default values (alignment, width, and so on) for all columns in the group at once.

COLS (attribute)

Compliance

Syntax

`<FRAMESET ROWS="value list" COLS="value list">...</FRAMESET>`

Definition

The `COLS` attribute of the `<FRAMESET>` tag controls the width and number of the frames in a browser's window. The value list can contain:

- an integer value - This value is the fixed size of the frame in pixels. Try not to use fixed sizes for all frame in a frame set because the user can change the size of the browser's window. If the browser window is too small or too large, the result is unpredictable.

- a percentage - This value is the percent of the overall height or width of the browser window to devote to a frame.

- * - The asterisk is used to create relative-sized frames. All remaining space not devoted to fixed-width or percentage frame is given to the relative-sized frame. If you have more than one relative-sized frame, the remaining space is split equally among them. You can also place a number in front of the asterisk, like "3*", to make one relative-size frame three times as big as another relative-sized frame.

When the COLS attribute is valued as "100, 200, *", the browser displays three vertical frames—a left frame 100 pixels wide, a middle frame 200 pixels wide, and a right frame that fills out the rest of the browser's window.

When the COLS attribute is valued as "20%, 10%, *", the browser displays three vertical frames—a left frame that uses 20 percent of the browser window, a middle frame that uses 10 percent of the browser window, and a right frame that fills out the rest of the browser's window.

Category

Frames

Example Syntax

```
<HTML>
 <HEAD>
  <TITLE>Eclectic Consulting Home Page</TITLE>
 </HEAD>
<FRAMESET COLS="150,*">
  <FRAME NORESIZE SCROLLING=Auto NAME="menu"
src="menu.html">
  <FRAME NORESIZE SCROLLING=Auto NAME="text"
src="welcome.html">
 </FRAMESET>
<NOFRAME>
  <P>I'm sorry but you have a frames-challenged web
browser.
  <P>Please connect directly to http://
www.affy.com/welcome.html
 </NOFRAME>
</HTML>
```

COLSPAN (attribute)

Compliance

Syntax

```
<TD ALIGN="alignment" COLSPAN="value"
  HEIGHT="numPixels" NOWRAP ROWSPAN="value"
  VALIGN="alignment" WIDTH="numPixels">...</TD>
```

Definition

The COLSPAN attribute of the `<TD>` and `<TH>` tags controls how many columns the current cell uses. Normally, cells default to a single column.

Category

Tables

Example Syntax

```
<!-- The table in this example looks like this:

*****************************************************
*          *      A Two Cell Row       *
*          *****************************************
*          * The Left Column * The Right Column *
* A Four Cell Row *********************************
*          * top left cell  * top right cell  *
*          *****************************************
*          * bottom left cell* bottom right cell*
*****************************************************
-->
<TABLE BORDER=5 CELLPADDING=5>
 <CAPTION>A Sample Table</CAPTION>
 <TR>
```

```
  <TH ROWSPAN=4>A Four Row Cell</TH>
  <TH COLSPAN=2>A Two Column Cell</TH>
</TR>
<TR>
 <TH>The left column</TH>
 <TH>The right column</TH>
</TR>
<TR>
 <TD>top left cell</TD>
 <TD>top right cell</TD>
</TR>
<TR>
 <TD>bottom left cell</TD>
 <TD>bottom right cell</TD>
</TR>
</TABLE>
```

COMMENT (obsolete)

Although Internet Explorer recognizes this tag, it is not standard. You should use the <!-- . . . --> form of the `<comment>` tag instead.

COMPACT (attribute)

Compliance

Syntax

```
<MENU COMPACT>...</MENU>
<OL COMPACT START="n" TYPE="type">...</OL>
```

Definition

The COMPACT attribute directs the browser to minimize spaces between individual items in a list. It does not seem to change the display in Netscape Navigator or Internet Explorer Web browsers.

Category

Lists

Example Syntax

```
<MENU COMPACT>
 <LI>One
 <LI>Two
 </MENU>
```

Related Elements

The COMPACT attribute can be used with the <DIR>, <MENU>, <OL>, and <UL> tags.

CONTENT (attribute)

Compliance

Syntax

```
<META NAME="name" CONTENT="content">
```

Definition

The CONTENT attribute is used to define the value of the NAME attribute. While there are a couple of standard names (see the Example Syntax), you can also create your own standards for name-value pairs.

Category

None

Example Syntax

```
<META NAME="REVIEWED-BY" CONTENT="Jack R. Adams">
<META NAME="DESCRIPTION" CONTENT="The best web page
for joggers!">
```

Related Elements

The CONTENT attribute is part of the <META> tag.

CONTROLS (attribute)

Compliance

Syntax

```
<IMG ALIGN="alignment" ALT="alternative text"
   BORDER="numPixels" CONTROLS HEIGHT="numPixels"
   DYNSRC="animation file" HSPACE="numPixels" ISMAP
   SRC="url of image file" USEMAP="url of map"
   VSPACE="numPixels" WIDTH="numPixels">
```

Definition

The CONTROLS attribute of the <IMG> tag controls the appearance of a start/stop button and a slider control bar below the display of an AVI file or video clip.

Category

Graphics

Example Syntax

```
<IMG ALT="[Animation of Whales]" BORDER=0
  CONTROLS DYNSRC="whales.avi">
```

COORDS (attribute)

Compliance

Syntax

```
<AREA SHAPE="shape" COORDS="x,y pairs">
```

Definition

The COORDS attribute is used in conjunction with the SHAPE attribute to define the clickable areas in an image map. The upper-left corner of the image is (0, 0).

Category

Links, Graphics

Example Syntax

```
<MAP NAME="menu">
<!-- #$AUTHOR:Purple Canyon Web Designs -->
<!-- #$DATE:Mon Jan 06 05:55:25 1997 -->
<!-- #$PATH:C:\web projects\Web
Projects\purplecanyon\images\ -->
<!-- #$GIF:rocks_h.jpg -->
<AREA SHAPE=CIRCLE COORDS="63,48,49"
HREF="graphix.html">
<AREA SHAPE=CIRCLE COORDS="133,126,48"
HREF="why.html">
<AREA SHAPE=CIRCLE COORDS="228,105,44"
HREF="clients.html">
```

```
<AREA SHAPE=RECT COORDS="134,182,239,249"
HREF="prices.html">
<AREA SHAPE=POLY
COORDS="10,148,23,227,111,203,45,123,10,148"
  HREF="contact.html">
<AREA SHAPE=default HREF="http://
www.purplecanyon.com">
</MAP>
<img src="images/rocks_h.jpg" width=265 height=261
  border=0 alt="Choose!!!!!" usemap=#menu>
```

CREDIT (not used)

The <CREDIT> tag was intended to name the source of a
<BLOCKQUOTE> or figure. It is not used.

DD

Compliance

Syntax

<DD>...</DD>

Definition

The <DD> tag is part of the formatting of a definition list. It displays an
indented definition below the term. Definition lists are useful in formatting multiple glossary or dictionary entries in an HTML document.

Category

Lists

Example Syntax

```
<DL>
<DT>affy</DT>
<DD>to confide or trust</DD>
<DD>to join closely</DD>
<DT>kingling</DT>
<DD>a small or petty king</DD>
<DT>orology</DT>
<DD>the science of mountains.</DD>
</DL>
```

NOTE   You can have more than one definition per item. And you can have more than one item per definition.

DEL (not used)

The `<DEL>` tag was intended to logically represent deleted text. For example, in modifications of multiple author documents.

DFN

Compliance

Syntax

```
<DFN>...</DFN>
```

Definition

The `<DFN>` tag identifies the *defining instance* of a word or term. The defining instance is the first time it is used. Internet Explorer displays the contents of the `<DFN>` tag in italic and Netscape Navigator does not emphasize the contents at all.

DIR

Compliance

Syntax

```
<DIR COMPACT>...</DIR>
```

Definition

The `<DIR>` tag creates a compact, narrow list. A common use for the `<DIR>` tag is in alphanumeric indexes of content. The `<DIR>` tag might constrain each item in the list to 20 characters, depending on which browser is used to view the Web page.

Category

Lists, Structural

Example Syntax

```
<DIR> <LI>NY Cities
<LI>Manhattan
<LI>Yonnkers
<LI>White Plains
<LI>Queens
<LI>Rochester</DIR>
```

DIV

Compliance

Syntax

```
<DIV ALIGN="alignment">...</DIV>
```

Definition

The `<DIV>` tag is currently used to set a default alignment. The default alignment can be set to LEFT, RIGHT, or CENTER.

Category

Structural

Example Syntax

```
<DIV ALIGN=RIGHT>
 <P>This is a test.</P>
 <DIV ALIGN=CENTER>
  <P>This is a test.</P>
  <DIV ALIGN=LEFT>
   <P>This is a test.</P>
  </DIV>
 </DIV>
</DIV>
```

DL

Compliance

Syntax

```
<DL COMPACT>...</DL>
```

Definition

The `<DL>` tag displays its contents as a list of terms and definitions, as in a glossary. The term is displayed flush left with the definition slightly indented. Terms are specified using the `<DD>` tag with its associated definition immediately following inside a `<DT>` tag. When `COMPACT` attribute is used, the list is displayed as compactly as possible.

Category

Lists

Example Syntax

```
<DL>
<DT>affy</DT>
<DD>to confide or trust</DD>
<DD>to join closely</DD>
<DT>kingling</DT>
<DD>a small or petty king</DD>
<DT>orology</DT>
<DD>the science of mountains.</DD>
</DL>
```

NOTE You can have more than one definition per item. And you can have more than one item per definition.

DOCTYPE

Compliance

Syntax

`<!DOCTYPE ...>`

Definition

The `<DOCTYPE>` tag is used by SGML (Standard General Markup Language) editors to detect what kind of document is being processed. The `<DOCTYPE>` tag always comes before the `<HTML>`, `<HEAD>` or `<BODY>` tags.

Category

None

Example Syntax

```
<!-- This is the doctype declaration for HTML 3.2 -->
<!DOCTYPE HTML PUBLIC "-//IETF//DTD HTML 3.2//EN">

<!-- This is the doctype declaration for HTML 2.0 -->
<!DOCTYPE HTML PUBLIC "-//IETF//DTD HTML 2.0//EN">
```

DT

Compliance

Syntax

```
<DT>...</DT>
```

Definition

The `<DT>` tag specifies a *definition term* in a definition list. All `<DT>` tags should have an associated `<DD>` tag. `<DD>` tags specify the definition descriptions. You can have more than one term per definition description.

Category

Lists

Example Syntax

```
<DL>
<DT>affy</DT>
<DD>to confide or trust</DD>
<DD>to join closely</DD>
<DT>kingling</DT>
<DD>a small or petty king</DD>
```

DT

```
<DT>orology</DT>
<DD>the science of mountains.</DD>
</DL>
```

NOTE   You can have more than one definition per item. And you can
have more than one item per definition.

DYNSRC (attribute)

Compliance

Syntax

```
<IMG CONTROLS DYNSRC="url of dynamic source">
```

Definition

The DYNSRC attribute specifies the location of a video, AVI clip, or
VRML world.

Category

None

Example Syntax

```
<IMG BORDER=0 ALT="[Animation of Whales]"
  CONTROLS DYNSRC="whales.avi">
```

EM

Compliance

Syntax

```
<EM>...</EM>
```

Definition

The `<EM>` tag directs the browser to represent the contents with some type of emphasis. The exact method of emphasis is left up to the browser. However, most browsers use italic.

Category

Structural

Example Syntax

```
<P>Of the following items, the <EM>first</EM> is
most important.
```

EMBED

Compliance

Syntax

```
<EMBED SRC="url" HEIGHT="numPixels"
WIDTH="numPixels" ...>
```

Definition

The `<EMBED>` tag inserts an arbitrary object into a Web page. The embedded objects are supported by application-specific plug-ins. The attributes used by the `<EMBED>` tag are defined by the plug-in creator.

Category

None

Example Syntax

```
<EMBED SRC="logo.mcf" WIDTH=350 HEIGHT=150>
 <NOEMBED>
  <P>Browsers that use the HotSauce plugin
  would be seeing a 3D version of the site.
 </NOEMBED>
</EMBED>
```

ENCTYPE (attribute)

Compliance

Syntax

```
<FORM ENCTYPE="type">
```

Definition

The ENCTYPE attribute controls how the form information is sent to the Web server or how it is sent using e-mail. The default value for the ENCTYPE attribute is "application/x-www-form-urlencoded". (If you'd like to know more about URL encoding, read *CGI by Example,* also published by Que.) Some browsers, such as Netscape Navigator, also support a value of "text/plain."

Category

Links and Graphics

Example Syntax

```
<!-- This version of the form only runs on Netscape
   Navigator, I think. -->
<FORM ACTION="mailto:user@foo.com"
  ENCTYPE="text/plain">
 Enter Name:
```

```
<INPUT TYPE="text" VALUE="David" NAME="First">
<INPUT TYPE="text" VALUE="Medinets" NAME="Last">
<INPUT TYPE="submit">
</FORM>

<!-- This version of the form should run on nearly
    every browser. -->
<FORM ACTION="http://www.foo.com/cgi-bin/
register.cgi"
  ENCTYPE="application/x-www-form-urlencoded">
 Enter Name:
 <INPUT TYPE="text" VALUE="David" NAME="First">
 <INPUT TYPE="text" VALUE="Medinets" NAME="Last">
 <INPUT TYPE="submit">
</FORM>
```

FIG (not used)

The <FIG> tag was proposed as a more advanced version of the <IMG> tag. It was originally intended to allow optional overlays, text elements, and hyperlinks. I believe that <FIG> has been superseded by client-side images (see the <MAP> tag).

FN (not used)

The <FN> tag was proposed as a way to represent footnotes.

FONT

Compliance

FONT

Syntax

```
<FONT COLOR="color" FACE="typeface"
SIZE="options">...</FONT>
```

Definition

The <FONT> tag provides the author with a means of customizing text with regard to font typeface, size, and color. The attributes used by the <FONT> tag are

- COLOR - The COLOR attribute controls the color the text is displayed in. You can specify the color by using color names (see the table under the COLOR entry) or you can use hexadecimal numbers to define the RGB value of the desired color (also described under the color entry).

- FACE - The FACE attribute is a nonstandard extension that both Netscape Navigator and Internet Explorer supports. Other browsers may support this tag. You can specify up to three typefaces in a comma-delimited list. The first installed typeface is used when the text is displayed. If the specified fonts are not installed, the browser uses its default font.

- SIZE - The SIZE attribute can range from 1 (smallest) to 7 (largest) or you can specify a relative size (like +1 or -1). Try to avoid large jumps in font size because they make your text hard to read. Instead of using <FONT SIZE=+1>, consider using <BIG>. Likewise, <SMALL> might be a better option than <FONT SIZE=-1>.

Category

Presentation

Example Syntax

```
<P><FONT FACE="Courier">Fixed-width Font</FONT>
<P><FONT COLOR="Red">This text is RED!</FONT>
<P><FONT COLOR=#ff0000>This text is RED!</FONT>
```

FORM

Compliance

Syntax

```
<FORM ACTION="url" METHOD="method"
  ENCTYPE="mime type">...</FORM>
```

Definition

The `<FORM>` tag provides a means of accepting input from the user and sending it to a Web server or to an e-mail address. Forms can include text input boxes, check boxes, option buttons, drop-down lists, and push buttons to make selections. All forms need to have at least one button called the submit button. When clicked, the submit button starts the transfer of form information to the server. Forms are allowed to have more than one submit button. The name of the submit button is sent along with the rest of the form information so the processing agent knows which button was clicked. The attributes of the `<FORM>` tag are

- ACTION - The `ACTION` tag specifies where the form information sent for processing. Usually, it is the URL of a CGI script. However, it can also be an e-mail address.
  (ACTION="**mailto:name@foo.com**"). I also have seen forms that have only one element—a push button— and use the URL to specify the next Web page to display.

- METHOD - The `METHOD` attribute can be valued GET or PUT. The GET option sends form information in an URL when the submit button is clicked. The PUT option sends the form information as a message when the submit button is clicked. For more information about forms and CGI processing, see Que's *CGI by Example*.

- ENCTYPE - The `ENCTYPE` attribute controls how the form information is sent to the Web server or how it is sent using e-mail. The default value for the `ENCTYPE` attribute is "application/x-www-form-urlencoded". (If you'd like to know more about

URL encoding, read *CGI by Example* published by Que.) Some browsers, such as Netscape Navigator, also support a value of "text/plain" (see Figure 2.2).

Category

Forms

Example Syntax

```
<FORM ACTION="http://www.customk9.com/ ~customk9/
cgi-bin/formmail.cgi" METHOD="post">
<input type="hidden" name="recipient"
value="rjanek@customk9.com">
<input type="hidden" name="subject" value="Invince-
A-Bell Order">
...
</FORM>
```

Related Elements

It doesn't make sense to have a form with no input fields. Therefore, HTML provides the <INPUT>, <SELECT>, and <TEXTAREA> tags.

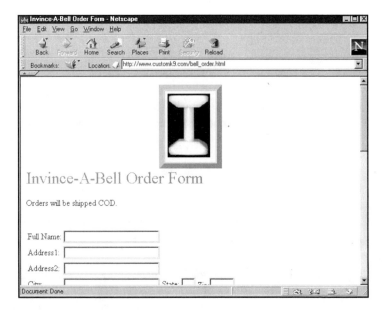

Fig. 2.2 This is an example of a form's drop-down list and text boxes.

FRAME

Compliance

Syntax

```
<FRAME NAME=" name" MARGINHEIGHT=" numPixels"
    MARGINWIDTH=" numPixels" NORESIZE
    SCROLLING=" options" SRC=" url">
```

Definition

The `<FRAME>` tag specifies a single frame in a set of frames. The attributes of the `<FRAME>` tag are

- NAME - The NAME attribute specifies the frame's name so that the TARGET attribute of the A tag can reference it.

- MARGINHEIGHT - The MARGINHEIGHT attribute controls the upper and lower margins of the frame. If not specified, the browser decides the appropriate margin. For smaller frames, set the MARGINHEIGHT to 1.

- MARGINWIDTH - The MARGINWIDTH attribute controls the left and right margins of the frame. If not specified, the browser decides the appropriate margin. For smaller frames, set the MARGINWIDTH to 1.

- NORESIZE - The NORESIZE attribute specifies that the user can't resize the frame. If not used, the user can change the frame size by dragging the frame border to the new location with the mouse.

- SCROLLING - The SCROLLING attribute can be valued "YES", "NO", and "AUTO". When the value is "YES", scrollbars are displayed. When the value is "NO", there are no scrollbars. And when the value is "AUTO", the scrollbars are displayed if the frame content is too much to see all at once.

- SRC - The SRC attribute is the URL of the Web page intended to be displayed in the frame. If not specified, the frame will be blank.

Category

Frames

Example Syntax

```
<HTML>
 <HEAD>
  <TITLE>Eclectic Consulting Home Page</TITLE>
 </HEAD>
 <FRAMESET COLS="150,*">
  <FRAME NORESIZE SCROLLING=Auto NAME="menu"
src="menu.html">
  <FRAME NORESIZE SCROLLING=Auto NAME="text"
src="welcome.html">
 </FRAMESET>
 <NOFRAME>
  <P>I'm sorry but you have a frames-challenged web
browser.
  <P>Please connect directly to http://
www.affy.com/welcome.html
 </NOFRAME>
</HTML>
```

FRAMESET

Compliance

Syntax

```
<FRAMESET ROWS="value list" COLS="value list">...</
FRAMESET>
```

Definition

The `<FRAMESET>` tag is used to create independent frames in the browser window. Each frame (defined by the `<FRAME>` tag) can display its own HTML page. The `<FRAMESET>` tag must be used in lieu of the `<BODY>` tag.

The basic `<FRAMESET>` tag can divide the browser window only in either rows or columns, not both. You must use the nested `<FRAMESET>` tag in order to create more complex frame layouts.

The `ROWS` and `COLS` attributes are a comma-delimited list of values that control the width and height of the frames. The value list can contain:

- an integer value - This value is the fixed size of the frame in pixels. Try not to use fixed sizes for all frames in a frame set because the user can change the size of the browser window. If the browser window is too small or too large, the result is unpredictable.

- a percentage - This value is the percent of the overall height or width of the browser window to devote to a frame.

- * - The asterisk is used to create relative-sized frames. All remaining space not devoted to a fixed-width or percentage frame is given to the relative-sized frame. If you have more than one relative-sized frame, the remaining space is split equally among them. You can also place a number in front of the asterisk, like "3*", to make one relative-size frame three times as big as another relative-sized frame.

When the `ROWS` attribute is valued as "100, 200, *", the browser displays three horizontal frames—a left frame 100 pixels wide, a middle frame 200 pixels wide, and a right frame that fills out the rest of the browser window.

When the `ROWS` attribute is valued as "20%, 10%, *", the browser displays three horizontal frames—a left frame that uses 20 percent of the browser window, a middle frame that uses 10 percent of the browser window, and a right frame that fills out the rest of the browser window.

The most difficult thing to understand when working with frames is that the ROWS attribute controls the width of the vertical frames, while the COLS attribute controls the height of the horizontal frames.

NOTE   You can find a frames tutorial on the Web at **http://www.newbie.net/frames/**. And you can find more by going to the HotBot search engine (**http://www.hotbot.com**) and searching for the words "Frames" and "Tutorials."

Category

Frames

Example Syntax

```
<frameset rows="23%,*" frameborder=NO border=1>
<frame name="header" scrolling="no"
marginheight="5" marginwidth="2" src="frame1.html">
<frameset cols="20%,*">
<frame name="buttons" scrolling="no"
marginheight="25" marginwidth="2"
src="frame2.html">
<frame name="body" scrolling="yes"
src="about.html">
</frameset>
</frameset>
```

Related Elements

The <NOFRAME> tag is used to control the display for frame-challenged browsers. See Figure 2.3 to witness frames in action.

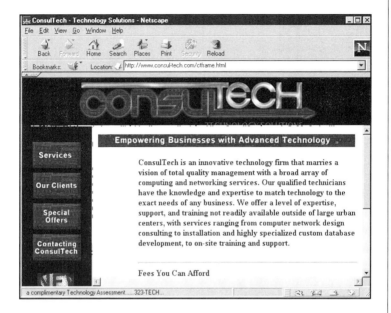

Fig. 2.3 The Consul-Tech Web site exhibits an exciting use of frames.

H1

Compliance

Syntax

`<H1 ALIGN="`*options*`">...</H1>`

Definition

The `<H1>` tag is the first level of heading (out of six possible levels) in your Web pages. It is usually displayed as the most prominent text available to the browser (i.e., a large, bold font). Most Web design books and authorities recommend using the different heading levels sequentially. For example, use H3 and then H4 instead of H3 and then H5.

Don't use heading level to emphasize, enlarge, embolden, or otherwise change the *look* of your Web pages. The heading levels should be used to add structure to your pages. Frequently, the heading levels are used by search engines and other automatic utilities to determine a table of contents for your Web page.

Try to avoid using other HTML tags inside heading text. Remember that automated tools might only be smart enough to recognize the heading tags. They probably won't be able to remove `<BR>` or `<P>` tags.

The `ALIGN` attribute can be valued as left, center, and right. It controls the horizontal alignment of the heading text, as seen in Figure 2.4.

Category

Structural

Example Syntax

```
<h1>Sean's personal projects</h1>
```

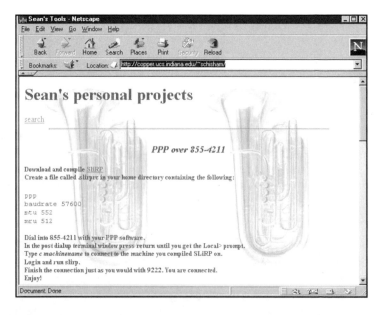

Fig. 2.4   The first-level heading, "Sean's personal projects," is shown in the largest available font.

H2

Compliance

Syntax

```
<H2 ALIGN="options">...</H2>
```

Definition

The `<H2>` tag is the second level of heading (out of six possible levels) in your Web pages. Most Web design books and authorities recommend using the different heading levels sequentially. For example, use `<H3>` and then `<H4>` instead of `<H3>` and then `<H5>`.

Don't use a heading level to emphasize, enlarge, embolden, or otherwise change the *look* of your Web pages. The heading levels should be used to add structure to your pages. Frequently, the heading levels are used by search engines and other automatic utilities to determine a table of contents for your Web page.

Try to avoid using other HTML tags inside heading text. Remember that automated tools might only be smart enough to recognize the heading tags. They probably won't be able to remove `<BR>` or `<P>` tags.

The `ALIGN` attribute can be valued as left, center, and right. It controls the horizontal alignment of the heading text.

Category

Structural

Example Syntax

```
<!-- In this example, all of the heading levels are
   used to create a highly structured page -->
<H1>Eclectic OnLine for September, 1997</H1>
 <H2>About the Magazine</H2>
 <H2>What's New!</H2>
```

```
<H3>Web Tools</H3>
 <H4>Unix</H4>
 <H4>Windows</H4>
  <H5>Web Server Software</H5>
   <H6>HTTP Servers</H6>
   <H6>FTP Servers</H6>
  <H5>Web Client Software</H5>
 <H3>Computer Languages</H3>
<H2>New and Notable Products</ H2>
```

H3

Compliance

Syntax

`<H3 ALIGN="`*options*`">...</H3>`

Definition

The `<H3>` tag is the third level of heading (out of six possible levels) in your Web pages. Most Web design books and authorities recommend using the different heading levels sequentially. For example, use `<H3>` and then `<H4>` instead of `<H3>` and then `<H5>`.

Don't use heading level to emphasize, enlarge, embolden, or otherwise change the *look* of your Web pages. The heading levels should be used to add structure to your pages. Frequently, the heading levels are used by search engines and other automatic utilities to determine a table of contents for your Web page.

Try to avoid using other HTML tags inside heading text. Remember that automated tools might only be smart enough to recognize the heading tags. They probably won't be able to remove `<BR>` or `<P>` tags.

The `ALIGN` attribute can be valued as left, center, and right. It controls the horizontal alignment of the heading text.

Category

Structural Definition

Example Syntax

```
<!-- In this example, all of the heading levels are
   used to create a highly structured page -->
<H1>Eclectic OnLine for September, 1997</H1>
 <H2>About the Magazine</H2>
 <H2>What's New!</H2>
  <H3>Web Tools</H3>
   <H4>Unix</H4>
   <H4>Windows</H4>
    <H5>Web Server Software</H5>
     <H6>HTTP Servers</H6>
     <H6>FTP Servers</H6>
    <H5>Web Client Software</H5>
  <H3>Computer Languages</H3>
 <H2>New and Notable Products</H2>
```

H4

Compliance

Syntax

```
<H4 ALIGN="options">...</H4>
```

Definition

The <H4> tag is the fourth level of heading (out of six possible levels) in your Web pages. Most Web design books and authorities recommend using the different heading levels sequentially. For example, use <H3> and then <H4> instead of <H3> and then <H5>.

Don't use heading level to emphasize, enlarge, embolden, or otherwise change the *look* of your Web pages. The heading levels should be used to add structure to your pages. Frequently, the heading levels are used by search engines and other automatic utilities to determine a table of contents for your Web page.

Try to avoid using other HTML tags inside heading text. Remember that automated tools might only be smart enough to recognize the heading tags. They probably won't be able to remove <BR> or <P> tags.

The ALIGN attribute can be valued as left, center, and right. It controls the horizontal alignment of the heading text.

Category

Structural Definition

Example Syntax

```
<!-- In this example, all of the heading levels are
    used to create a highly structured page -->
<H1>Eclectic OnLine for September, 1997</H1>
 <H2>About the Magazine</H2>
 <H2>What's New!</H2>
  <H3>Web Tools</H3>
   <H4>Unix</H4>
   <H4>Windows</H4>
    <H5>Web Server Software</H5>
     <H6>HTTP Servers</H6>
     <H6>FTP Servers</H6>
    <H5>Web Client Software</H5>
  <H3>Computer Languages</H3>
 <H2>New and Notable Products</H2>
```

H5

Compliance

Syntax

`<H5 ALIGN="`*`options`*`">...</H5>`

Definition

The `<H5>` tag is the fifth level of heading (out of six possible levels) in your Web pages. Most Web design books and authorities recommend using the different heading levels sequentially. For example, use `<H3>` and then `<H4>` instead of `<H3>` and then `<H5>`.

Don't use heading level to emphasize, enlarge, embolden, or otherwise change the *look* of your Web pages. The heading levels should be used to add structure to your pages. Frequently, the heading levels are used by search engines and other automatic utilities to determine a table of contents for your Web page.

Try to avoid using other HTML tags inside heading text. Remember that automated tools might only be smart enough to recognize the heading tags. They probably won't be able to remove `<BR>` or `<P>` tags.

The `ALIGN` attribute can be valued as left, center, and right. It controls the horizontal alignment of the heading text.

Category

Structural Definition

Example Syntax

```
<!-- In this example, all of the heading levels are
   used to create a highly structured page -->
<H1>Eclectic OnLine for September, 1997</H1>
 <H2>About the Magazine</H2>
 <H2>What's New!</H2>
  <H3>Web Tools</H3>
   <H4>Unix</H4>
   <H4>Windows</H4>
    <H5>Web Server Software</H5>
     <H6>HTTP Servers</H6>
     <H6>FTP Servers</H6>
    <H5>Web Client Software</H5>
  <H3>Computer Languages</H3>
 <H2>New and Notable Products</H2>
```

H6

Compliance

Syntax

`<H6 ALIGN="`*`options`*`">...</H6>`

Definition

The `<H6>` tag is the sixth level of heading (out of six possible levels) in your Web pages. Most Web design books and authorities recommend using the different heading levels sequentially. For example, use `<H3>` and then `<H4>` instead of `<H3>` and then `<H5>`.

Don't use heading level to emphasize, enlarge, embolden, or otherwise change the *look* of your Web pages. The heading levels should be used to add structure to your pages. Frequently, the heading levels are used by search engines and other automatic utilities to determine a table of contents for your Web page.

Try to avoid using other HTML tags inside heading text. Remember that automated tools might only be smart enough to recognize the heading tags. They probably won't be able to remove `<BR>` or `<P>` tags.

The `ALIGN` attribute can be valued as left, center, and right. It controls the horizontal alignment of the heading text.

Category

Structural Definition

Example Syntax

```
<!-- In this example, all of the heading levels are
    used to create a highly structured page -->
<H1>Eclectic OnLine for September, 1997</H1>
 <H2>About the Magazine</H2>
 <H2>What's New!</H2>
```

```
<H3>Web Tools</H3>
 <H4>Unix</H4>
 <H4>Windows</H4>
  <H5>Web Server Software</H5>
   <H6>HTTP Servers</H6>
   <H6>FTP Servers</H6>
  <H5>Web Client Software</H5>
 <H3>Computer Languages</H3>
<H2>New and Notable Products</H2>
```

HEAD

Compliance

Syntax

```
<HEAD>...</HEAD>
```

Definition

The <HEAD> tag contains HTML tags *about* the Web page. For example, the <TITLE> and <META> tags are found inside the <HEAD> tag. In addition, many Webmasters place JavaScript and VBScript functions inside the <HEAD> tag to ensure they are defined when the body of the page is displayed.

Category

Structural

Example Syntax

```
<HTML>
 <HEAD>
  <TITLE>CoolBlue! ... Your Watchdog Computer
Magazine</TITLE>
```

```
  <META NAME="GENERATOR" content="Mozilla/2.01Gold
(Win32)">
  </HEAD>
  <BODY>
  <H1>This is a short page</H1>
  </BODY>
</HTML>
```

Related Elements

The ⟨BASE⟩, ⟨ISINDEX⟩, ⟨LINK⟩, ⟨META⟩, ⟨SCRIPT⟩, ⟨STYLE⟩, and ⟨TITLE⟩ tags can be contained inside the ⟨HEAD⟩ tag.

HPn (not used)

The set of HP*n* (where n=1,2,...) tags provided a way to highlight characters in a phrase. This tag is no longer part of the HTML standard and is obsolete.

HR

Compliance

Syntax

```
<HR ALIGN="alignment" NOSHADE SIZE="numPixels"
WIDTH="value">
```

Definition

The ⟨HR⟩ tag draws a shaded, center-justified horizontal rule by default. You can use the following attributes with the ⟨HR⟩ tag:

- ALIGN - The ALIGN attribute controls the alignment of the horizontal rule. It can be valued as LEFT, CENTER, and RIGHT.
- NOSHADE - When present, the NOSHADE attribute displays a simple line with the 3-D shading effects.
- SIZE - The SIZE attribute controls the height or thickness of the horizontal line.
- WIDTH - The WIDTH attribute controls how wide the horizontal line is. You can specify a specific number of pixels or you can specify a percent of the browser window.

CAUTION   Percentages must be specified in quotes!

Category

None

Example Syntax

```
<P>This is the first paragraph in the
example. In order to separate it from
next paragraph a horizontal line is
used.</P>
<HR WIDTH=50%>
<P>This is the second paragraph in
the example.</P>
```

HREF (attribute)

Compliance

Syntax

```
<A HREF="url" NAME="anchor">...</A>
```

Definition

The HREF attribute of the <A> tag specifies where the browser goes when the link is clicked. You can use any valid URL as the target (see Table 2.2).

Category

Links

Example Syntax

Table 2.2   Common URL Types

URL Type	URL Example
CGI Script	http://www.codebits.com/cgi-bin/test.pl
	http://www.codebits.com/cgi-bin/test.cgi
Gopher Servers	gopher://www.codebits.com
Intra-Page Link	http://www.codebits.com#Section Two
JavaScript	javascript:*javascript script*
Telnet	telnet://www.codebits.com
UseNet Newsgroup	news:comp.lang.perl.misc
WAIS Server	wais://www.codebits.com
Web Page	http://www.codebits.com
E-mail	mailto:medined@planet.net
	mailto:medined@planet.net?Subject=HTML Ref

CAUTION   Not all Web browsers support the *Subject* option in the mailto URL.

Related Elements

The NAME attribute of the <A> tag is used to create intra-page URLs. Intra-page URLs are mentioned in the entry for <A>.

HSPACE (attribute)

Compliance

Syntax

```
<IMG ALIGN="alignment" ALT="alternative text"
   BORDER="numPixels" HEIGHT="numPixels"
   HSPACE="numPixels" ISMAP
   SRC="url of image file" USEMAP="url of map"
   VSPACE="numPixels" WIDTH="numPixels">
<MARQUEE ALIGN="alignment" BEHAVIOR="options"
     BGCOLOR="color" DIRECTION="direction"
     HEIGHT="numPixels" HSPACE="numPixels"
     LOOP="options" SCROLLAMOUNT="numPixels"
     SCROLLDELAY="numMilliseconds"
     VSPACE="numPixels"
     WIDTH="numPixels">...</MARQUEE>
```

Definition

The HSPACE attribute is used by the <IMG> and <MARQUEE> tags. It controls the amount of blank space that buffers the image from other elements on the left and right sides of the image or marquee.

Category

Graphics

Example Syntax

```
<IMG BORDER=0 HSPACE=10 SRC="logo.gif">
```

HTML

Compliance

Syntax

```
<HTML VERSION="version">...</HTML>
```

Definition

The `<HTML>` tag, when used, is the outermost tag. It is not required. If used, any `<DOCTYPE>` tags are placed *before* the `<HTML>` tag in the document and all other tags must be contained inside the `<HTML>` tag.

Category

Structural

Example Syntax

```
<HTML>
  <HEAD>
   <TITLE>The Example Page</TITLE>
  </HEAD>
 <BODY>
  <H1>The Example Heading</H1>
 </BODY>
</HTML>
```

HTTP-EQUIV (attribute)

Compliance

Syntax

```
<META HTTP-EQUIV="options" CONTENT="options">
```

Definition

The HTTP-EQUIV attribute of the <META> tag specifies response headers for the Web page. When the Web page is requested by a Web server, the HTTP-EQUIV values should be sent as part of the HTTP response.

There are two popular values for the HTTP-EQUIV attribute. When you set equal to "refresh" you can force the browser to load a different page—also called Web-page *redirection*. Redirection is valuable if you have rearranged your Web site. The first following example shows how this is done.

When the HTTP-EQUIV is set to "expires" and the current date is after the specified date, the browser should load a new copy of the Web page instead of reading the Web page from its cache. The second example that follows shows how this is done.

Category

None

Example Syntax

```
<!-- Web Page Redirection -->

<!-- This page is http://www.affy.com/CodeBits/.
However,
    I've moved the contents of the page to
    http://www.codebits.com so when the user arrives
at this page, I want them to be automatically
redirected
    to the new page. -->
<!DOCTYPE HTML PUBLIC "-//W3C//DTD HTML 3.2//EN">
<HTML>
<HEAD>
  <TITLE> Perl CodeBits </TITLE>
  <!-- Wait 5 seconds and the redirection -->
  <META HTTP-EQUIV=refresh CONTENT="5; URL=http://
www.codebits.com">
</HEAD>
```

```
<BODY>
<!-- Displaying this message and allowing the user
five
   seconds to read it should ensure that the user
   updates their bookmarks.
<H1 ALIGN=CENTER>Perl CodeBits<BR> has moved to<BR>
<A HREF="http://www.codebits.com">http://
www.codebits.com</A>.</H1>

<P>If you're lucky, the new page will automatically
replace this one in five seconds. Otherwise, please
click on the above hypertext link.
</BODY>
</HTML>

<!-- Forcing Web Page Reload -->

<!-- In this example, I want the user to reload the
web page at the end of the month because new pric-
ing will
   be needed them.
<!DOCTYPE HTML PUBLIC "-//W3C//DTD HTML 3.2//EN">
<HTML>
 <HEAD>
  <META HTTP-EQUIV="expires" CONTENT="Tue, 31 Jan
1997 01:00:00 GMT">
  <TITLE> Jack's Catalog </TITLE>
 </HEAD>
 <BODY>
 </BODY>
</HTML>
```

I

Compliance

Syntax

`<I>...</I>`

Definition

The `<I>` tag displays its contents in an italic or slanted font. Older (and non-graphic) browsers might not use an italic font. However, you are guaranteed the font used will be different from that used with the `<B>` tag (see Figure 2.5).

Category

Presentation

Example Syntax

```
<H2><I>Add yourself to the database (890+
strong!)</I></H2>
```

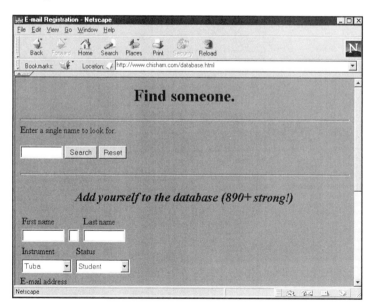

Fig. 2.5   Frequently, Webmasters use italic to display instructions.

ID (unused attribute)

The <ID> attribute was intended to be part of the <A> tag. It was part of a failed attempt to add tab stops into the HTML standard.

IMG

Compliance

Syntax

```
<IMG ALIGN="alignment" ALT="alternative text"
   BORDER="numPixels" CONTROLS DYNSRC="animation
file"
   HEIGHT="numPixels" HSPACE="numPixels" ISMAP
LOOP="options"
   SRC="url of image file" USEMAP="url of map"
   VSPACE="numPixels" WIDTH="numPixels">
```

Definition

The <IMG> tag displays a specified image. The attributes for the <IMG> tag are:

- ALIGN - The ALIGN attribute can be valued as LEFT, RIGHT, TOP, MIDDLE, and BOTTOM. The LEFT and RIGHT values display the images flush to the appropriate browser edge and let the text of the page flow around the image. The TOP, MIDDLE, and BOTTOM control the vertical alignment of the image with the line of text.

- ALT - The value of the ALT attribute is displayed when the image is not displayed. Many people surf the Internet and set their browser to not display images. This speeds up the downloading of Web pages. Because the alternative text is displayed when the images are not, it is a really good idea to always use the ALT attribute.

- BORDER - The BORDER attribute is used when the image is a link (when it is surrounded by the `<A HREF>..</A> tag`). Normally, a narrow border surrounds the image so the user knows the image is a link. You can turn off the border by setting the BORDER attribute to zero. When BORDER is zero, the image itself should indicate that it is clickable.

- CONTROLS - The Microsoft Explorer-specific CONTROLS attribute controls the appearance of a start/stop button and a slider control bar below the display of an AVI file or video clip.

- DYNSRC - The Microsoft Explorer-specific DYNSRC attribute specifies the URL of an animation file.

- HEIGHT - The HEIGHT attribute specifies the image height in pixels.

- HSPACE - The HSPACE attribute controls the amount of blank space that "buffers" the image from other elements on the left and right sides of the image.

- ISMAP - The ISMAP attribute indicates the image is a server-side image map and when clicked, the Web server will process the coordinates of the mouse pointer's location.

- LOOP - The LOOP attribute plays a sound while the page is active (`LOOP=INFINITE`) or plays a sound some number of seconds (`LOOP=n`, where n is the number of seconds).

- SRC - The SRC attribute specifies the graphic file to display.

- USEMAP - The USEMAP attribute indicates the image is a client-side image map. An example of client-side image maps is shown in the entry for the `<MAP>` tag.

- VSPACE - The VSPACE attribute controls the amount of blank space that buffers the image from other elements on the top and bottom sides of the image.

- WIDTH - The WIDTH attribute specifies the image width in pixels.

You can use the HEIGHT and WIDTH attributes to resize the image. For example, if the actual image dimensions are 100x100, you can specify a height and width of 50 in order to shrink the image in half.

It is considered good manners to *always* use the HEIGHT and WIDTH attributes, because modern browsers display bordered rectangles as the image downloads. In addition, browsers will display the text of the Web page faster (see Figure 2.6).

Category

Graphics

Example Syntax

```
<IMG SRC="PENTRANS.GIF" ALT="Army Field Band Unit
Crest" WIDTH=168 HEIGHT=126 ALIGN=top>
```

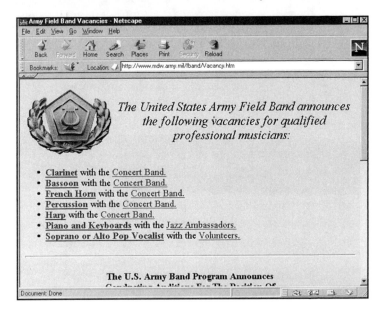

Fig. 2.6 The United States Army Field Band logo is displayed using the `<IMG>` tag.

INPUT

Compliance

Syntax

```
<INPUT ALIGN="alignment" CHECKED MAXLENGTH="value"
    NAME="name" SIZE="value" SRC="url of image
file"
    TYPE="field type" VALUE="value">
```

Definition

The `<INPUT>` tag is used to add input fields to a form—each input field requires its own `<INPUT>` tag. The `TYPE` attribute controls which kind of input field is added for each `<INPUT>` tag. You can add text, check boxes, radio buttons, submit buttons, and reset buttons. Some newer browsers support uploading files, also.

When a submit button is clicked, the form information is processing according to the `METHOD` and `ACTION` attributes of the enclosing `<FORM>` tag. You can use more than one submit button on a form as long as their NAME attributes are different.

When a reset button is clicked, all input fields are reset to their default values.

The `<INPUT>` tag has the following attributes:

- ALIGN - The `ALIGN` attribute can be valued as LEFT, RIGHT, TOP, MIDDLE, and BOTTOM. It is only valid when the `TYPE` attribute is `IMAGE`. The LEFT and RIGHT values control the horizontal alignment while the TOP, MIDDLE, and BOTTOM values control the vertical alignment of the image.

- CHECKED - The `CHECKED` attribute is only valid for check box and radio button input fields. Check boxes and radio buttons have two states, checked and not checked—which correlate to "on" and "off." When the `CHECKED` attribute is present, the input field is displayed in the "on" state.

- MAXLENGTH - The `MAXLENGTH` attribute is only valid for text and password input fields. When present, the user can only enter `MAXLENGTH` characters into the input field. However, remember the user can create a local, modified copy of the form so don't depend on seeing only `MAXLENGTH` characters. If `MAXLENGTH` is greater than `SIZE`, the text scrolls left and right as needed.

- NAME - The `NAME` attribute is required and is associated with the value of the input field when the form data is sent to the Web server.

- SIZE - The `SIZE` attribute is only valid for text and password input fields. It controls the size of the input box, not how many characters can be entered.

- SRC - The `SRC` attribute is only valid for image fields. It is the URL of the graphic file to be displayed. Image fields act like submit buttons when clicked. The x and y positions of the mouse pointer are also sent as part of the form information so image fields can act like server-side image maps.

- TYPE - The `TYPE` attribute controls the type of input field that is added to the form. You can value the `TYPE` attribute as `TEXT`, PASSWORD, CHECKBOX, RADIO, SUBMIT, RESET, FILE, HIDDEN, and IMAGE. When not specified, an input type of `TEXT` is used. Password fields usually display asterisks instead of the actual letters typed into the field. Radio buttons are grouped together according to their names. Each radio button should have a different value so that the form processing agent can tell them apart. File input fields are used to upload files from the local hard disk to the Web server. Because of security limitations, you can't provide a default value for file input fields. Hidden fields are used to pass information to the form processing agent, which is not seen by the form user. Image fields are like submit buttons except they display an image.

- VALUE - The `VALUE` attribute provides the default value for the input field. When a reset button is clicked, the default values provided in the `VALUE` attributes (if any) are redisplayed.

Category

Forms

Example Syntax

```
<HTML>
 <HEAD>
 </HEAD>
 <BODY>

 <!-- The CustomerNum field is hidden to add conve-
 nience for the customer and to minimize the infor-
 mation
```

```
    that is displayed on the form. -->
 <FORM ACTION="http://www.affy.com/cgi-bin/test.pl>
  <INPUT TYPE="hidden" NAME="CustomerNum"
VALUE="AZ123">

  <!-- A table is used to ensure that all visible
form element are automatically aligned in an es-
thetic way -->
  <TABLE BORDER=5 CELLPADDING=5>
   <TR>
    <TD>Name:</TD>
    <TD><INPUT TYPE="TEXT" NAME="Name" SIZE=45></
TD>
   </TR>
   <TR>
    <TD>Phone Number:</TD>
    <TD><INPUT TYPE="TEXT" NAME="Address"
SIZE=45></TD>
   </TR>
  </TABLE>
 </FORM>
 </BODY>
</HTML>
```

Related Elements

All <INPUT> tags must be inside <FORM> tags. Forms can also use <SELECT> and <TEXTAREA> tags.

INS (not used)

The <INS> tag was intended to represent inserted text. It never made it into the HTML 3.2 standard.

ISINDEX

Compliance

Syntax

```
<ISINDEX PROMPT=" string" >
```

Definition

The `<ISINDEX>` tag is generally inserted into a Web page by the Web server, not the Webmaster. It was used before the `<FORM>` tag became popular.

CAUTION Simply inserting the `<ISINDEX>` tag does not make a Web page searchable. The searching is only done with Web server support.

Category

None

Example Syntax

```
<ISINDEX PROMPT="Enter keywords into input field below">
```

Related Elements

Use the `<FORM>` tag instead of the `<ISINDEX>` tag.

ISMAP (attribute)

Compliance

Syntax

```
<IMG ALIGN="alignment" ALT="alternative text"
   BORDER="numPixels" CONTROLS HEIGHT="numPixels"
   DYNSRC="animation file" HSPACE="numPixels" ISMAP
   SRC="url of image file" USEMAP="url of map"
   VSPACE="numPixels" WIDTH="numPixels">
```

Definition

The ISMAP attribute of the <IMG> indicates the image is a server-side image map and when clicked, the Web server will process the coordinates of the mouse pointer's location.

In order to create an image map in HTML the following <IMG> tag must be surrounded by an <A> tag whose HREF points to a MAP file. MAP files are used to assign an URL to each point of an image. You can find out more about image maps at the following:

http://www2.ncsu.edu/bae/people/faculty/walker/hotlist/ imagemap.html

Category

Graphics, Links

Example Syntax

```
<A HREF="logo.map "><IMG SRC="logo.gif"  ISMAP></A>
```

KBD

Compliance

Syntax

```
<KBD>...</KDB>
```

Definition

The ⟨KBD⟩ tag is frequently used in reference materials to indicate that the user needs to perform some keyboard-entry task. Normally, browsers display the text in a bold, fixed-width font.

Category

Structural

Example Syntax

```
<P>You can run Perl using the <KBD>perl -w
test.pl</KBD> command.</P>
```

LANG (not used)

The LANG tag was intended to change the human language used for subsequent Web page elements. It never made it into the HTML 3.2 standard.

LH (not used)

The ⟨LH⟩ tag was intended to define a list header used as a title for a list. It never made it into the HTML 3.2 standard.

LI

Compliance

Syntax

```
<LI TYPE="options" VALUE="value">..</LI>
```

Definition

The $\langle LI \rangle$ tag defines a list item. $\langle LI \rangle$ tags are contained within $\langle DIR \rangle$, $\langle MENU \rangle$, $\langle OL \rangle$, and $\langle UL \rangle$ tags. When contained within $\langle OL \rangle$ tags, the list items are displayed preceded by numbers. The TYPE attribute can valued as a number, a lowercase letter, an uppercase letter, or a Roman numeral. The VALUE attribute controls where the numbering starts from.

When contained within $\langle UL \rangle$ tags, the list items are displayed preceded by bullets. The TYPE attribute can be valued as DISC, SQUARE, or CIRCLE. The TYPE attribute controls which type of bullet is displayed (see Figure 2.7).

Category

Structural

Example Syntax

```
<li><a href="welcome.htm">Welcome message</a> from
Jeff Funderburk, President, TUBA
```

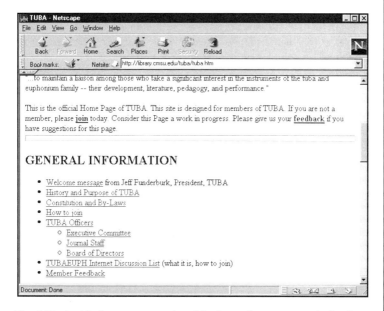

Fig. 2.7 In this figure, an unordered list is used to present a bullet list of general information.

LINK

Compliance

Syntax

```
<LINK HREF=" url" REL=" string" REV=" string"
TITLE=" title">
```

Definition

The `<LINK>` tag is not widely used yet. It is intended to provide enough information so that the Web browsers can create basic navigational toolbars by providing relational information about two Web pages. The REL attribute specifies a relation type between the current document and the one specified by the HREF attribute. The REV attribute specified an inverse relation—the relationship the other document has with the current one. Table 2.3 lists possible values for the REL and REV attributes. Possibly, the future will bring additional values as the navigational needs of Webmasters become better known.

Table 2.3   Possible Values for the *REL* and *REV* Attributes

Value	Description
made	The e-mail address of the Web page's creator—in the form of a mailto: URL.
stylesheet	The URL of the style sheet associated with the current Web document.
home	The URL of the home page for the Web site.
toc	The URL of the Table of Contents page for the Web site.
index	The URL of the Index page for the Web site.
glossary	The URL of the Glossary page for the Web site.
copyright	The URL of the copyright page for the Web site.

Value	Description
up	The URL of the Web page above the current Web page.
next	The URL of the Web page that precedes the current Web page.
previous	The URL of the Web page that logically follows the current Web page.
help	The URL of the Web page that documents the Web site or the current Web page.

Category

Meta-Information

Example Syntax

```
<HTML>
 <HEAD>
  <TITLE>What's New at CodeBits!</TITLE>
 </HEAD>
 <BODY>
  <LINK REL="home" HREF="http://www.codebits.com">
 </BODY>
</HTML>
```

LISTING

Compliance

Syntax

```
<LISTING WIDTH="numCharacters">...</LISTING>
```

Definition

The <LISTING> tag is still supported by most browsers; however, it is no longer part of the HTML standard. It has been replaced by the <PRE> tag. It was intended to represent multiline computer code listings.

Category

Structural

Example Syntax

```
<!-- The following listing is a Perl function
    to add two numbers. -->
<LISTING>
sub add {
 my($a, $b) = @_;
 $a + b$;
}
</LISTING>
```

LOOP (attribute of the BGSOUND tag)

Compliance

Syntax

```
<BGSOUND SRC=" url of sound file " LOOP=" options ">
```

Definition

The LOOP attribute of the <BGSOUND> tag plays a sound while the page is active (LOOP=" INFINITE") or plays a sound for a certain number of seconds ("LOOP=n", where n is the number of seconds).

Category

None

Example Syntax

```
<BGSOUND SRC="mozart.wav" LOOP="INFINITE">
```

LOOP (attribute of the IMG and MARQUEE tags)

Compliance

Syntax

```
<IMG ALIGN="alignment" ALT="alternative text"
   BORDER="numPixels" CONTROLS DYNSRC="animation
file"
   HEIGHT="numPixels" HSPACE="numPixels" ISMAP
LOOP="options"
   SRC="url of image file" USEMAP="url of map"
   VSPACE="numPixels" WIDTH="numPixels">
```

```
<MARQUEE ALIGN="alignment" BEHAVIOR="options"
     BGCOLOR="color" DIRECTION="direction"
     HEIGHT="value" HSPACE="numPixels"
     LOOP="options" SCROLLAMOUNT="numPixels"
     SCROLLDELAY="numMilliseconds"
     VSPACE="numPixels"
     WIDTH="numPixels">...</MARQUEE>
```

Definition

The LOOP attribute of the <IMG> and <MARQUEE> tags repeats its action continuously while the page is active (LOOP="INFINITE") or repeats the action a specific number of times ("LOOP=n", where n is the number of times to repeat).

LOOP (attribute of the IMG and MARQUEE tags)

Category

None

Example Syntax

```
<IMG DYNSRC="wavingFlads.avi" LOOP="INFINITE">
<MARQUEE DIRECTION="LEFT" LOOP="5">This text will
scroll to the left.</MARQUEE>
```

MAP

Compliance

Syntax

```
<MAP NAME="name">...</MAP>
```

Definition

The `<MAP>` tag specifies a collection of hot spots (clickable areas) for a client-side image map. The `NAME` attribute is referenced by the `USEMAP` attribute of the `<IMG>` tag.

You create a client-side image map by using the `<AREA>` tag to create clickable areas built out of rectangles, circles, and polygons.

Category

Graphics, Links

Example Syntax

You can see the following example in action at **http://www.purplecanyon.com**. Notice that comments are used to document the `<MAP>` tag.

```
<MAP NAME="menu">
```

```
<!-- #$AUTHOR:Purple Canyon Web Designs -->
<!-- #$DATE:Mon Jan 06 05:55:25 1997 -->
<!-- #$PATH:C:\web projects\Web
Projects\purplecanyon\images\ -->
<!-- #$GIF:rocks_h.jpg -->
<AREA SHAPE=CIRCLE COORDS="63,48,49"
HREF="graphix.html">
<AREA SHAPE=CIRCLE COORDS="133,126,48"
HREF="why.html">
<AREA SHAPE=CIRCLE COORDS="228,105,44"
HREF="clients.html">
<AREA SHAPE=RECT COORDS="134,182,239,249"
HREF="prices.html">
<AREA SHAPE=POLY
COORDS="10,148,23,227,111,203,45,123,10,148"
   HREF="contact.html">
<AREA SHAPE=default HREF="http://
www.purplecanyon.com">
</MAP>
<img src="images/rocks_h.jpg" width=265 height=261
   border=0 alt="Choose!!!!!" usemap=#menu>
```

Related Elements

The `<AREA>` tag is used to create clickable areas inside the `IMAGE`. The `<IMG>` tag is used to display an image and link the image to the `<MAP>` tag via the `USEMAP` attribute.

MARGINHEIGHT (attribute)

Compliance

Syntax

```
<FRAME NAME="name" MARGINHEIGHT="numPixels"
   MARGINWIDTH=" numPixels" NORESIZE
   SCROLLING=" options" SRC="url">
```

Definition

The MARGINHEIGHT attribute of the <FRAME> tag determines how much *vertical* space (in pixels) exists between the frame's content and the top and bottom inside edges of that frame. If not specified, the browser determines the appropriate MARGINHEIGHT. The smallest allowable margin is one pixel.

Category

Frames

Example Syntax

```
<FRAME NORESIZE MARGINHEIGHT=5 SCROLLING=Auto
  NAME="menu" src="menu.html">
```

MARGINWIDTH (attribute)

Compliance

Syntax

```
<FRAME NAME="name" MARGINHEIGHT="numPixels"
  MARGINWIDTH="numPixels" NORESIZE
  SCROLLING="options" SRC="url">
```

Definition

The MARGINWIDTH attribute of the <FRAME> tag determines how much *horizontal* space (in pixels) exists between the frame's content and the left or right inside edges of that frame. If not specified, the browser determines the appropriate MARGINHEIGHT. The smallest allowable margin is one pixel.

Category

Frames

Example Syntax

```
<FRAME NORESIZE MARGINWIDTH=5 SCROLLING=Auto
 NAME="menu" src="menu.html">
```

MARQUEE

Compliance

Syntax

```
<MARQUEE ALIGN=" alignment" BEHAVIOR=" options"
    BGCOLOR=" color" DIRECTION=" direction"
    HEIGHT=" value" HSPACE=" numPixels"
    LOOP=" options" SCROLLAMOUNT=" numPixels"
    SCROLLDELAY=" numMilliseconds"
    VSPACE=" numPixels"
    WIDTH=" numPixels">...</MARQUEE>
```

Definition

The Microsoft Internet Explorer-specific <MARQUEE> tag creates a scrolling text marquee displaying the contents of the tag. Attributes of the <MARQUEE> tag are

- ALIGN - The ALIGN attribute controls the vertical alignment of the text in the marquee. It can be valued as TOP, MIDDLE, and BOTTOM.

- BEHAVIOR - The BEHAVIOR attribute controls how the text moves. When valued as "SLIDE", the text scrolls into the marquee and then stops. When valued as "ALTERNATE", the text bounces from side to side. When valued as "SCROLL" (the default), the text continuously scrolls across the marquee.

- BGCOLOR - The BGCOLOR attribute controls the background color of the marquee. You can either use text-based color names, such as RED, GREEN, or BLUE, or you can specify colors as hexadecimal numbers. The list of color names is located in the "HTML Reference Tables" section of this book.

- DIRECTION - The `DIRECTION` attribute makes the text scroll either LEFT or RIGHT.
- HEIGHT - The `HEIGHT` attribute specifies the height of the marquee in either pixels or a percentage of the entire screen height.
- HSPACE - The `HSPACE` attribute controls the amount of blank space that buffers the image from other elements on the left and right sides of the marquee.
- LOOP - The `LOOP` attribute continuously scrolls the text while the page is active (`LOOP="INFINITE"`) or repeats the scroll a specific number of times (`"LOOP=n"`, where n is the number of times to repeat).
- SCROLLAMOUNT - The `SCROLLAMOUNT` attribute specifies the number of blank pixels between scroll repetitions.
- SCROLLDELAY - The `SCROLLDELAY` attribute specifies the time between scrolls in milliseconds.
- VSPACE - The `VSPACE` attribute controls the amount of blank space that buffers the image from other elements on the top and bottom sides of the marquee.
- WIDTH - The `WIDTH` attribute specifies the width of the marquee in either pixels or a percentage of the entire screen width.

Category

None

Example Syntax

```
<MARQUEE DIRECTION="LEFT">This text will scroll to
the left.</MARQUEE>
```

MAXLENGTH (attribute)

Compliance

Syntax

```
<INPUT ALIGN="alignment" CHECKED MAXLENGTH="value"
    NAME="name" SIZE="value" SRC="url of image
file"
    TYPE="field type" VALUE="value">
```

Definition

The MAXLENGTH attribute of the <INPUT> tag is valid only for text and password input fields. When present, the user can enter only MAXLENGTH characters into the input field. However, remember that the user can create a local, modified copy of the form, so don't depend on seeing only MAXLENGTH characters. If MAXLENGTH is greater than SIZE, the text scrolls left and right as needed.

Category

Forms

Example Syntax

```
<INPUT TYPE="TEXT" NAME="Address" SIZE=20
MAXLENGTH=60>
```

MENU

Compliance

Syntax

```
<MENU COMPACT>...</MENU>
```

Definition

The <MENU> tag displays a list of items—it is usually displayed more compactly than the UL lists. The <LI> tag is used to specify the beginning of each item in the menu list.

MENU

Category

Structural

Example Syntax

```
<MENU>
 <LI>Beef
 <LI>Pork
 <LI>Chicken
</MENU>
```

META

Compliance

Syntax

```
<META CONTENT="value" HTTP-EQUIV="options"
NAME="options">
```

Definition

The <META> tag can be used to specify information *about* the Web page, or it can be used to specify HTTP headers for the Web page. <META> tags are always contained inside the <HEAD> tag. The attributes of the <META> tag are:

- CONTENT - The CONTENT attribute changes format depending on the value of the HTTP-EQUIV or NAME attributes.

- HTTP-EQUIV - The HTTP-EQUIV attribute specifies response headers for the Web page. When the Web page is requested by a Web server, the HTTP-EQUIV values should be sent as part of the HTTP response.

- NAME - The NAME attribute determines which type of information is contained in the CONTENT attribute. For example, if the

NAME attribute is valued "description," then the CONTENT attribute would hold a short description of the Web page suitable for display in a search engine.

There are two popular values for the HTTP-EQUIV attribute. When it's set equal to "refresh," you can force the browser to load a different page—also called Web-page redirection. Redirection is valuable if you have rearranged your Web site. The first following example shows how this is done.

When the HTTP-EQUIV is set to "expires" and the current date is after the specified date, the browser should load a new copy of the Web page instead of reading the Web page from its cache. The following example shows how this is done.

The NAME attribute has no fixed values according to the HTML standard; however, some common values include:

- AUTHOR - The AUTHOR value indicates the Web page author's name.
- GENERATOR - The GENERATOR value indicates that the Web page was created automatically and is the name of the creation program.
- KEYWORDS - The KEYWORDS value is a list of comma-delimited words and phrases that search engines (such as InfoSeek or AltaVista) use to categorize and index your page.
- DESCRIPTION - The DESCRIPTION value is a short description of your Web page. Some search engines display this description when your page matches a keyword query.

Category

Structural

Example Syntax

```
<!-- Web Page Redirection -->

<!-- This page is http://www.affy.com/CodeBits/.
However,
    I've moved the contents of the page to
    http://www.codebits.com so when the user arrives
at
```

```
    this page, I want them to be automatically
redirected to the new page. -->
<!DOCTYPE HTML PUBLIC "-//W3C//DTD HTML 3.2//EN">
<HTML>
<HEAD>
  <TITLE> Perl CodeBits </TITLE>
  <META NAME="author" CONTENT="David Medinets">
  <!-- Wait 5 seconds and the redirection -->
  <META HTTP-EQUIV=refresh CONTENT="5; URL=http://
www.codebits.com">
</HEAD>
<BODY>
<!-- Displaying this message and allowing the user
five seconds to read it should ensure that the user
updates their bookmarks.
<H1 ALIGN=CENTER>Perl CodeBits<BR> has moved to<BR>
<A HREF="http://www.codebits.com">http://
www.codebits.com</A>.</H1>

<P>If you're lucky, the new page will automatically
replace this one in five seconds. Otherwise, please
click on the above hypertext link.
</BODY>
</HTML>

<!-- Forcing Web Page Reload -->

<!-- In this example, I want the user to reload the
web page at the end of the month because new pric-
ing will be needed them.
<!DOCTYPE HTML PUBLIC "-//W3C//DTD HTML 3.2//EN">
<HTML>
 <HEAD>
  <META NAME="generator" CONTENT="Jack's Automatic
Catalog">
  <META HTTP-EQUIV="expires" CONTENT="Tue, 31 Jan
```

```
1997 01:00:00 GMT">
  <TITLE> Jack's Catalog </TITLE>
 </HEAD>
 <BODY>
 </BODY>
 </HTML>
```

METHOD (attribute)

Compliance

Syntax

```
<FORM ACTION="url" METHOD="method"
  ENCTYPE="mime type">...</FORM>
```

Definition

The METHOD attribute of the <FORM> tag can be valued GET or PUT. The GET option sends form information in an URL when the submit button is clicked. The PUT option sends the form information as a message when the submit button is clicked. For more information about forms and CGI processing, see *CGI by Example*, published by Que.

Category

Forms

Example Syntax

```
<!-- This version of the form only runs on Netscape
  Navigator, I think. -->
<FORM ACTION="mailto:user@foo.com"
  ENCTYPE="text/plain">
 Enter Name:
```

```
 <INPUT TYPE="text" VALUE="David" NAME="First">
 <INPUT TYPE="text" VALUE="Medinets" NAME="Last">
<INPUT TYPE="submit">
</FORM>


<!-- This version of the form should run on nearly
    every browser. -->
<FORM ACTION="http://www.foo.com/cgi-bin/
register.cgi"
  ENCTYPE="application/x-www-form-urlencoded">
 Enter Name:
 <INPUT TYPE="text" VALUE="David" NAME="First">
 <INPUT TYPE="text" VALUE="Medinets" NAME="Last">
<INPUT TYPE="submit">
</FORM>
```

Related Elements

It doesn't make sense to have a form with no input fields. Therefore, HTML provides the `<INPUT>`, `<SELECT>`, and `<TEXTAREA>` tags.

MULTIPLE (attribute)

Compliance

Syntax

```
<SELECT MULTIPLE NAME="name"
    SIZE="numVisibleItems">...<SELECT>
```

Definition

The MULTIPLE attribute of the <SELECT> tag, when used, lets multiple selections be chosen in the list box.

Category

Forms

Example Syntax

```
<FORM>
 <SELECT NAME="bookCategory" MULTIPLE>
  <OPTION SELECTED>Science Fiction</OPTION>
  <OPTION>History</OPTION>
  <OPTION>Cooking</OPTION>
  <OPTION>Self-Help</OPTION>
 </SELECT>
</FORM>
```

NAME (attribute of the A tag)

Compliance

Syntax

```
<A HREF="url" NAME="anchor">...</A>
```

Definition

The NAME attribute of the <A> tag indicates that the elements inside the <A> tag can be a target for an HREF. In other words, the NAME attribute creates an intra-page anchor. If you have
<A NAME="Testing"><H2>Testing</H2></A> in a file called bar.html, then you can jump directly to that H2 heading using
<A HREF="bar.html#Testing">Link to Testing Section</A>.

Category

Links

Example Syntax

```
<A NAME="First Heading"><H1>First Heading</H1></A>
<P>This is a paragraph.</P>
<A NAME="Second Heading"><H1>Second Heading</H1></
A>
<P>This is another paragraph. Click <A HREF="#First
Heading">here</A>
to return to the first heading.</P>
```

The "here" text under the second heading is a hyperlink back to the first heading. The pound sign is used to reference NAME targets inside Web pages. URLs refer to the whole Web page and NAMEs refer to the anchors indicated by the <A> tag.

NAME (attribute of the FRAME tag)

Compliance

Syntax

```
<FRAME NAME="name" MARGINHEIGHT="numPixels"
   MARGINWIDTH="numPixels" NORESIZE
   SCROLLING="options" SRC="url">
```

Definition

The NAME attribute of the <FRAME> tag specifies the frame's name so that the TARGET attribute of the <A> tag can reference it.

Category

Frames

Example Syntax

```
<FRAME NORESIZE MARGINWIDTH=5 SCROLLING=Auto
  NAME="menu" src="menu.html">
```

Related Elements

Frames are targeted using the TARGET attribute of the <A> tag.

NAME (attribute of the MAP tag)

Compliance

Syntax

```
<MAP NAME="name">...</MAP>
```

Definition

The NAME attribute of the <MAP> tag creates a reference usable by the USEMAP attribute of the <IMG> tag.

Category

Links

Example Syntax

You can see the following example in action at **http://www.purplecanyon.com**. Notice that comments are used to document the <MAP> tag.

```
<MAP NAME="menu">
 <!-- #$AUTHOR:Purple Canyon Web Designs -->
 <!-- #$DATE:Mon Jan 06 05:55:25 1997 -->
 <!-- #$PATH:C:\web projects\Web
```

```
Projects\purplecanyon\images\ -->
 <!-- #$GIF:rocks_h.jpg -->
 <AREA SHAPE=CIRCLE COORDS="63,48,49"
HREF="graphix.html">
 <AREA SHAPE=CIRCLE COORDS="133,126,48"
HREF="why.html">
 <AREA SHAPE=CIRCLE COORDS="228,105,44"
HREF="clients.html">
 <AREA SHAPE=RECT COORDS="134,182,239,249"
HREF="prices.html">
 <AREA SHAPE=POLY
COORDS="10,148,23,227,111,203,45,123,10,148"
   HREF="contact.html">
 <AREA SHAPE=default HREF="http://
www.purplecanyon.com">
 </MAP>
<img src="images/rocks_h.jpg" width=265 height=261
   border=0 alt="Choose!!!!!" usemap=#menu>
```

Related Elements

The <AREA> tag is used to create clickable areas inside the IMAGE. The <IMG> tag is used to display an image and link the image to the <MAP> tag via the USEMAP attribute.

NAME (attribute of the META tag)

Compliance

Syntax

```
<META CONTENT="value" HTTP-EQUIV="options"
NAME="options">
```

Definition

The NAME attribute of the `<META>` tag determines which type of information is contained in the CONTENT attribute. For example, if the NAME attribute is valued "description" then the CONTENT attribute would hold a short description of the Web page suitable for display in a search engine.

The NAME attribute has no fixed values according to the HTML standard; however, some common values include:

- AUTHOR - The AUTHOR value indicates the Web page author's name.
- GENERATOR - The GENERATOR value indicates that the Web page was created automatically and is the name of the creation program.
- KEYWORDS - The KEYWORDS value is a list of comma-delimited words and phrases that search engines (such as InfoSeek or AltaVista) use to categorize and index your page.
- DESCRIPTION - The DESCRIPTION value is a short description of your Web page. Some search engines display this description when your page matches a keyword query.

NAME (attribute of the SELECT tag)

Compliance

Syntax

```
<SELECT MULTIPLE NAME="name"
    SIZE="numVisibleItems">...<SELECT>
```

Definition

The NAME attribute of the `<SELECT>` tag is used to identify the input field in scripting languages, by CGI programs, or by other form processing agents.

Category

Forms

Example Syntax

```
<FORM>
 <SELECT NAME="bookCategory">
  <OPTION SELECTED>Science Fiction</OPTION>
  <OPTION>History</OPTION>
  <OPTION>Cooking</OPTION>
  <OPTION>Self-Help</OPTION>
 </SELECT>
</FORM>
```

NEXTID (not used)

The proposed `<NEXTID>` tag was intended to provide the next available identifier for automatic hypertext editors. It has been superseded by the `<LINK>` tag.

NOBR (obsolete)

Compliance

Syntax

```
<NOBR>...</NOBR>
```

Definition

The `<NOBR>` tag turns off word-wrapping when displays its contents. This tag, while supported, is no longer part of the HTML standard. It has been superseded by the `<PRE>` tag.

Category

Presentation

Example Syntax

```
<P>For great tips on how to program, visit
<NOBR>http://www.codebits.com </NOBR>.
```

NOEMBED

Compliance

Syntax

```
<NOEMBED>...</NOEMBED>
```

Definition

The Netscape Navigator-specific `<NOEMBED>` tag displays its contents if the browser is not capable of supporting embedded objects.

Category

None

Example Syntax

```
<EMBED SRC="logo.mcf" WIDTH=350 HEIGHT=150>
 <NOEMBED>
  <P>Browsers that use the HotSauce plugin
  would be seeing a 3-D version of the site.
 </NOEMBED>
</EMBED>
```

NOFRAMES

Compliance

Syntax

```
<NOFRAMES>...</NOFRAMES>
```

Definition

The `<NOFRAMES>` tag display its contents if the browser is not capable of supporting frames.

Category

Frames

Example Syntax

```
<HTML>
 <HEAD>
  <TITLE>Eclectic Consulting Home Page</TITLE>
 </HEAD>
 <FRAMESET COLS="150,*">
  <FRAME NORESIZE SCROLLING=Auto NAME="menu"
src="menu.html">
  <FRAME NORESIZE SCROLLING=Auto NAME="text"
src="welcome.html">
 </FRAMESET>
 <NOFRAME>
  <P>I'm sorry but you have a frames-challenged web
browser.
  <P>Please connect directly to http://
www.affy.com/welcome.html
 </NOFRAME>
</HTML>
```

NOHREF (attribute)

Compliance

Syntax

```
<AREA ALT="alternate text"
   COORDS="coordinates"
   HREF="url"
   NOHREF
   SHAPE="shape">
```

Definition

The NOHREF attribute of the <AREA> tag indicates that no links should be generated by the area.

Category

Graphics, Links

Example Syntax

```
<AREA SHAPE=CIRCLE COORDS="63,48,49" NOHREF>
```

Related Elements

The <AREA> tag is only allowed inside of <MAP> tags. In addition, <MAP> tags are useless without a related <IMG USEMAP=" map name"> tag.

NORESIZE (attribute)

Compliance

Syntax

```
<FRAME NAME="name" MARGINHEIGHT="numPixels"
    MARGINWIDTH="numPixels" NORESIZE
    SCROLLING="options" SRC="url">
```

Definition

The NORESIZE attribute of the <FRAME> tag specifies that the user can't resize the frames. If not used, the user can change the frame size by dragging the frame border to the new location with the mouse. By default, all frames are resizable.

Category

Frames

Example Syntax

```
<HTML>
 <HEAD>
  <TITLE>Eclectic Consulting Home Page</TITLE>
 </HEAD>
 <FRAMESET COLS="150,*">
  <FRAME NORESIZE SCROLLING=Auto NAME="menu"
src="menu.html">
  <FRAME NORESIZE SCROLLING=Auto NAME="text"
src="welcome.html">
 </FRAMESET>
 <NOFRAME>
  <P>I'm sorry but you have a frames-challenged web
browser.
  <P>Please connect directly to http://
www.affy.com/welcome.html
 </NOFRAME>
</HTML>
```

NOSHADE (attribute)

Compliance

Syntax

```
<HR ALIGN="alignment" NOSHADE SIZE="numPixels"
WIDTH="value">
```

Definition

The NOSHADE is attribute of the <HR> tag. When present, it displays a simple line with the 3-D shading effects.

Category

Structural

Example Syntax

```
<P>This is the first paragraph in the
example. In order to separate it from
next paragraph a horizontal line is
used.</P>
<HR NOSHADE SIZE=10 WIDTH=50%>
<P>This is the second paragraph in
the example.</P>
```

NOTE (not used)

The <NOTE> tag was intended to represent Notes, Cautions, and Warnings. It never made it into the HTML 3.2 standard.

NOWRAP (attribute)

Compliance

Syntax

```
<TD ALIGN="alignment" COLSPAN="value"
  HEIGHT="numPixels" NOWRAP ROWSPAN="value"
  VALIGN="alignment" WIDTH="numPixels">...</TD>
```

Definition

The NOWRAP attribute of the <TD> and <TH> tags, when present, displays the cell contents as a single line. The <BR> tag is used to force a line break as needed.

Category

Tables

OL

Compliance

Syntax

```
<OL COMPACT START="n" TYPE="type">...</OL>
```

Definition

The <OL> tag indicates the beginning of an ordered list. An ordered list displays each list item with a sequentially increased number or letter. The attributes of the <OL> tag are

- COMPACT - The COMPACT attribute directs the browser to minimize spaces between individual items in a list. It does not seem to change the display in Netscape Navigator or Internet Explorer Web browsers.
- START - The START attribute specifies the beginning number or letter to start the list with.
- TYPE - The TYPE attribute controls when numbers or letters are used to order the list. The valid values are "1", "a", "A", "i", and "I".

Not all Web browsers support the START and TYPE attributes.

Category

Lists

Example Syntax

```
<OL>
 <LI>List item one.
 <LI>List item two.
</OL>
```

Related Elements

The list items are specified using the <LI> tag.

OPTION

Compliance

2   3   3.2

Syntax

```
<OPTION SELECTED VALUE="value">...</OPTION>
```

Definition

The `<OPTION>` tag defines an item in a list box or drop-down list input field on a form. All `<OPTION>` tags are contained inside `<SELECT>` tags. The SELECTED attribute, when present, indicates that this option is initially selected when the list is first displayed. You can pre-select multiple options if the MULTIPLE attribute is used in the `<SELECT>` tag.

Category

Forms

Example Syntax

```
<FORM>
 <SELECT NAME="bookCategory">
  <OPTION SELECTED>Science Fiction</OPTION>
  <OPTION>History</OPTION>
  <OPTION>Cooking</OPTION>
  <OPTION>Self-Help</OPTION>
 </SELECT>
</FORM>
```

Related Elements

All `<OPTION>` tags must be contained inside `<SELECT>` tags which must be contained inside `<FORM>` tags.

OVERLAY (not used)

The `<OVERLAY>` tag was intended to create image overlays. This tag is no longer part of the HTML standard and is obsolete.

P

Compliance

Syntax

```
<P ALIGN="alignment">...</P>
```

Definition

The `<P>` tag logically represents a single paragraph. The `ALIGN` attribute controls the horizontal alignment of the paragraph—valid values are `LEFT`, `CENTER`, and `RIGHT`.

Category

Structural Definition

Example Syntax

```
<P>We encourage you to contact us with your
comments and suggestions. If you provide us with
your contact information, we will be able to reach
you should we have any questions.</P>
```

PARAM

Compliance

Syntax

```
<PARAM NAME="name" VALUE="value">
```

Definition

The `<PARAM>` tag is used to supply parameters to Java applets. All `<PARAM>` tags are contained inside `<APPLET>` tags. The `NAME` attribute is the name of the parameter. The `VALUE` attribute is the value of the parameter.

Category

None

Example Syntax

```
<APPLET CODE="RDispMain.class" CODEBASE="rundisp"
WIDTH=500 HEIGHT=45>
 <PARAM NAME=MESG VALUE="'Four Score and
Seven...'">
</APPLET>
```

PERSON (not used)

The <PERSON> tag was intended to represent an individual's name. This tag is no longer part of the HTML standard and is obsolete.

PLAINTEXT (not used)

The <PLAINTEXT> tag was used to force browsers to ignore HTML code in Web pages. It has been superseded by the <PRE> tag. This tag is no longer part of the HTML standard and is obsolete.

PRE

Compliance

Syntax

```
<PRE WIDTH="numCharacters">...</PRE>
```

Definition

The $\langle PRE \rangle$ tag displays its contents exactly as shown in the HTML source code—usually in a fixed-width font. This essentially means that new lines in the Web page will be displayed as new lines in the browser and that word-wrap is turned off.

HTML presentation tags are still active. You must use HTML entities (see the section "HTML Reference Tables") in order to display certain characters. For example, the < character should be referred to as < and the > character should be referred to as >.

The $\langle WIDTH \rangle$ tag is not widely supported, but it is supposed to indicate the width of the widest line. Some browsers use $\langle WIDTH \rangle$ to determine the display font size.

You can't include image or font size changes inside the $\langle PRE \rangle$ tags.

Category

Presentation

Example Syntax

```
<PRE>The PRE tag is
good for situations,
like poetry, that need
narrow columns.</PRE>
```

PROMPT (attribute)

Compliance

Syntax

```
<ISINDEX PROMPT="string" >
```

Definition

The PROMPT attribute of the <ISINDEX> tag displays a customized message. The <ISINDEX> tag has been largely superseded by the <FORM> tag.

Category

Forms

Example Syntax

```
<ISINDEX PROMPT="Enter keywords into input field
below">
```

Q (not used)

The proposed <Q> tag was intended to represent quoted text. The tag was never approved as part of any HTML standard and is not used.

ROWS (attribute)

Compliance

Syntax

```
<FRAMESET ROWS="value list" COLS="value list">...</
FRAMESET>
```

Definition

The ROWS attribute of the <FRAMESET> tag controls the width and number of frames in the browser window. The value list can contain:

- an integer value - This value is the fixed size of the frame in pixels. Try not to use fixed sizes for all frames in a frame set because the user can change the size of the browser window. If the browser window is too small or too large, the result is unpredictable.

- a percentage - This value is the percent of the overall height or width of the browser window to devote to a frame.

- * - The asterisk is used to create relative-sized frames. All remaining space not devoted to fixed-width or percentage frame is given to the relative-sized frame. If you have more than one relative-sized frame, the remaining space is split equally among them. You can also place a number in front of the asterisk, like "3*", to make one relative-size frame three times as big as another relative-sized frame.

When the ROWS attribute is valued as "100, 200, *", the browser displays three horizontal frames—a left frame 100 pixels wide, a middle frame 200 pixels wide, and a right frame that fills out the rest of the browser window.

When the ROWS attribute is valued as "20%, 10%, *", the browser displays three horizontal frames—a left frame that uses 20 percent of the browser window, a middle frame that uses 10 percent of the browser window, and a right frame that fills out the rest of the browser window.

Category

Frames

Example Syntax

```
<HTML>
 <HEAD>
  <TITLE>Eclectic Consulting Home Page</TITLE>
 </HEAD>
 <FRAMESET ROWS="150,*">
  <FRAME NORESIZE SCROLLING=Auto NAME="menu"
src="menu.html">
  <FRAME NORESIZE SCROLLING=Auto NAME="text"
src="welcome.html">
 </FRAMESET>
 <NOFRAME>
```

```
   <P>I'm sorry but you have a frames-challenged web
browser.
   <P>Please connect directly to http://
www.affy.com/welcome.html
 </NOFRAME>
</HTML>
```

ROWSPAN (attribute)

Compliance

Syntax

```
<TD ALIGN="alignment" COLSPAN="value"
  HEIGHT="numPixels" NOWRAP ROWSPAN="value"
  VALIGN="alignment" WIDTH="numPixels">...</TD>
```

Definition

The ROWSPAN attribute of the <TD> and <TH> tags controls how many rows the current cell uses. Normally, cells default to a single row.

Category

Frames

Example Syntax

```
<!-- The table in this example looks like this:

*************************************************************
*           *       A Two Cell Row         *
*           *****************************************
*           *  The Left Column * The Right Column *
* A Four Cell Row  ****************************
```

```
*          * top left cell  * top right cell  *
*          ***********************************
*          * bottom left cell* bottom right cell*
*****************************************************
-->
<TABLE BORDER=5 CELLPADDING=5>
 <CAPTION>A Sample Table</CAPTION>
 <TR>
  <TH ROWSPAN=4>A Four Row Cell</TH>
  <TH COLSPAN=2>A Two Column Cell</TH>
 </TR>
 <TR>
  <TH>The left column</TH>
  <TH>The right column</TH>
 </TR>
 <TR>
  <TD>top left cell</TD>
  <TD>top right cell</TD>
 </TR>
 <TR>
  <TD>bottom left cell</TD>
  <TD>bottom right cell</TD>
 </TR>
</TABLE>
```

S (obsolete)

The <S> tag was used to display text with a strikeout line. It has been superseded by the <STRIKE> tag. This tag is no longer part of the HTML standard and is obsolete.

SAMP

Compliance

Syntax

```
<SAMP>...</SAMP>
```

Definition

The `<SAMP>` tag is used to indicate literal output from a program. It is usually displayed in a fixed-width font, but there are no guarantees. If you need a fixed-width font, use the `<TT>` or `<PRE>` tags.

Category

Structural

Example Syntax

```
<P>The program continuously printed
<SAMP>David Was Here!</SAMP> to the screen.</P>
```

SCROLLING (attribute)

Compliance

Syntax

```
<FRAME NAME=" name" MARGINHEIGHT=" numPixels"
    MARGINWIDTH=" numPixels" NORESIZE
    SCROLLING=" options" SRC=" url">
```

Definition

The SCROLLING attribute of the `<FRAME>` tag controls the display of scrollbars in the frame. It can be valued as "YES", "NO", and "AUTO". When the value is "YES", scrollbars are displayed. When the value is "NO", there are no scrollbars. And when the value is "AUTO", the scrollbars are displayed if the frame content is too much to see all at once.

Category

Frames

Example Syntax

```
<HTML>
 <HEAD>
  <TITLE>Eclectic Consulting Home Page</TITLE>
 </HEAD>
 <FRAMESET COLS="150,*">
  <FRAME NORESIZE SCROLLING=Auto NAME="menu"
src="menu.html">
  <FRAME NORESIZE SCROLLING=Auto NAME="text"
src="welcome.html">
 </FRAMESET>
 <NOFRAME>
  <P>I'm sorry but you have a frames-challenged web
browser.
  <P>Please connect directly to http://
www.affy.com/welcome.html
 </NOFRAME>
</HTML>
```

SCRIPT

Compliance

Syntax

```
<SCRIPT>...</SCRIPT>
```

Definition

The `<SCRIPT>` tag is used to enclose scripting languages like JavaScript or Visual Basic Script. Some browsers don't recognize the

<SCRIPT> tag so it is a good idea to enclose your scripts inside comments. For more information about scripting, read *JavaScript by Example* or *VBScript by Example*, also published by Que.

Category

None

SELECT

Compliance

Syntax

```
<SELECT MULTIPLE NAME="name"
    SIZE="numVisibleItems">...<SELECT>
```

Definition

The <SELECT> tag defines a drop-down list box input field on a form. All <SELECT> tags are contained inside <FORM> tags. The items inside the list box are added by using <OPTION> tags as the contents of the <SELECT> tag. The attributes of the <SELECT> tag are

- MULTIPLE - The MULTIPLE attribute, when used, lets multiple selections be chosen in the list box.
- NAME - The NAME attribute is required and is associated with the value of the input field when the form data is sent to the Web server.
- SIZE - The SIZE attribute controls how many items are visible when the list box is displayed.

Category

Forms

Example Syntax

```
<FORM>
 <SELECT NAME="bookCategory">
  <OPTION SELECTED>Science Fiction</OPTION>
  <OPTION>History</OPTION>
  <OPTION>Cooking</OPTION>
  <OPTION>Self-Help</OPTION>
 </SELECT>
</FORM>
```

SHAPE (attribute)

Compliance

Syntax

```
<AREA ALT="alternate text" COORDS="coordinates"
   HREF="url" NOHREF SHAPE="shape">
```

Definition

The SHAPE attribute of the <AREA> tag specifies the geometric shape that the <AREA> tag is defining. The <AREA> tag is used to define a clickable area on a client-side image map. Valid values are RECT, CIRCLE, POLY, and DEFAULT. The default shape covers the whole image map and is used to provide a default hyperlink.

Category

Graphics, Links

Example Syntax

You can see the following example in action at **http://www.purplecanyon.com**. Notice that the author has intelligently used comments to document the <MAP> tag.

```
<MAP NAME="menu">
 <!-- #$AUTHOR:Purple Canyon Web Designs -->
 <!-- #$DATE:Mon Jan 06 05:55:25 1997 -->
 <!-- #$PATH:C:\web projects\Web
Projects\purplecanyon\images\ -->
 <!-- #$GIF:rocks_h.jpg -->
 <AREA SHAPE=CIRCLE COORDS="63,48,49"
HREF="graphix.html">
 <AREA SHAPE=CIRCLE COORDS="133,126,48"
HREF="why.html">
 <AREA SHAPE=CIRCLE COORDS="228,105,44"
HREF="clients.html">
 <AREA SHAPE=RECT COORDS="134,182,239,249"
HREF="prices.html">
 <AREA SHAPE=POLY
COORDS="10,148,23,227,111,203,45,123,10,148"
   HREF="contact.html">
 <AREA SHAPE=default HREF="http://
www.purplecanyon.com">
</MAP>
<img src="images/rocks_h.jpg" width=265 height=261
  border=0 alt="Choose!!!!!" usemap=#menu>
```

Related Elements

The <AREA> tag is only allowed inside of <MAP> tags. In addition,
<MAP> tags are useless without a related
<IMG USEMAP="*map name*"> tag.

SIZE (attribute of the FONT tag)

Compliance

Syntax

```
<FONT COLOR="color" FACE="typeface"
SIZE="options">...</FONT>
```

Definition

The SIZE attribute of the <FONT> tag can range from 1 (smallest) to 7 (largest) or you can specify a relative size (like +1 or -1). Try to avoid large jumps in font size because they make your text hard to read. Instead of using <FONT SIZE=+1>, consider using <BIG>. Likewise, <SMALL> might be a better option than <FONT SIZE=-1>.

Category

Structural Definition

Example Syntax

```
<FONT SIZE=7>This text is displayed in the largest
font size.</FONT>
```

SIZE (attribute of the INPUT tag)

Compliance

Syntax

```
<INPUT ALIGN=" alignment" CHECKED MAXLENGTH=" value"
    NAME=" name" SIZE=" value" SRC=" url of image
file"
    TYPE=" field type" VALUE=" value">
```

Definition

The SIZE attribute of the <INPUT> tag controls the length of a text or password input field.

Category

Forms

Example Syntax

```
<FORM ACTION="http://www.foo.com/cgi-bin/
register.cgi"
  ENCTYPE="application/x-www-form-urlencoded">
 Enter Name:
 <INPUT TYPE="text" VALUE="David" NAME="First"
SIZE=15>
 <INPUT TYPE="text" VALUE="Medinets" NAME="Last"
SIZE=20>
<INPUT TYPE="submit">
</FORM>
```

Related Elements

All `<INPUT>` tags must be inside `<FORM>` tags. Forms can also use `<SELECT>` and `<TEXTAREA>` tags.

SIZE (attribute of the SELECT tag)

Compliance

Syntax

```
<SELECT MULTIPLE NAME="name"
    SIZE="numVisibleItems">...<SELECT>
```

Definition

The `SIZE` attribute of the `<SELECT>` tag controls how many items are visible when the list box is displayed.

Category

Forms

Example Syntax

```
<FORM>
 <SELECT NAME="bookCategory" SIZE=3>
  <OPTION SELECTED>Science Fiction</OPTION>
  <OPTION>History</OPTION>
  <OPTION>Cooking</OPTION>
  <OPTION>Self-Help</OPTION>
 </SELECT>
</FORM>
```

SMALL

Compliance

Syntax

```
<SMALL>...</SMALL>
```

Definition

The `<SMALL>` tag decreases the font size of text by one size.

Category

Presentation

Example Syntax

```
<P><SMALL>Small</SMALL> is beautiful!</P>
```

SOUND

Compliance

Syntax

```
<SOUND DELAY=" numSeconds" LOOP=" options"
    SRC="url of wav file">
```

Definition

The Mosaic-specific <SOUND> tag plays a .wav sound file. The attributes of the <SOUND> tag are

- DELAY - The DELAY attribute delays the playing of the sound file by a specified number of seconds.
- LOOP - The LOOP attribute, when set to INFINITE, plays the .wav file continuously.

Category

None

Example Syntax

```
<SOUND SRC="COOL_SOUND.WAV" LOOP=INFINITE DELAY=1>
```

Related Elements

The <BGSOUND> tag is slightly more portable because both Mosaic and Internet Explorer recognize it.

SPAN (not used)

The <SPAN> tag was intended to change the human language used for its contents. It never made it into the HTML 3.2 standard.

SRC (attribute of the FRAME tag)

Compliance

Syntax

```
<FRAME NAME=" name" MARGINHEIGHT=" numPixels"
    MARGINWIDTH=" numPixels" NORESIZE
    SCROLLING=" options" SRC=" url">
```

Definition

The SRC attribute of the <FRAME> tag is the URL to be displayed in the frame. If not specified, the frame will be blank.

Category

Frames

Example Syntax

```
<HTML>
 <HEAD>
  <TITLE>Eclectic Consulting Home Page</TITLE>
 </HEAD>
 <FRAMESET COLS="150,*">
  <FRAME NORESIZE SCROLLING=Auto NAME="menu"
src="menu.html">
  <FRAME NORESIZE SCROLLING=Auto NAME="text"
src="welcome.html">
 </FRAMESET>
 <NOFRAME>
  <P>I'm sorry but you have a frames-challenged web
browser.
  <P>Please connect directly to http://
```

```
www.affy.com/welcome.html
  </NOFRAME>
</HTML>
```

SRC (attribute of the IMAGE tag)

Compliance

Syntax

```
<IMG ALIGN="alignment" ALT="alternative text"
   BORDER="numPixels" CONTROLS DYNSRC="animation
file"
   HEIGHT="numPixels" HSPACE="numPixels" ISMAP
LOOP="options"
   SRC="url of image file" USEMAP="url of map"
   VSPACE="numPixels" WIDTH="numPixels">
```

Definition

The SRC attribute of the <IMG> tag specifies the graphic file to display.

Category

Graphics

Example Syntax

```
<IMG SRC="logo.gif">
```

STRIKE

Compliance

Syntax

`<STRIKE>...</STRIKE>`

Definition

The `<STRIKE>` tag displays text with a strikeout line. This tag is relatively new and is not supported by all browsers yet.

Category

Presentation

Example Syntax

`<STRIKE>This text will have a line bisecting it!`
`</STRIKE>`

STRONG

Compliance

Syntax

`<STRONG>...<STRONG>`

Definition

The <STRONG> tag indicates strongly emphasized text. The text is displayed in such a way as to make it more emphatic than text surrounded by the <EM> tag.

Category

Structural

Example Syntax

```
<STRONG>Most browsers to display this text in BOLD
type!</STRONG>
```

STYLE

Compliance

Syntax

```
<STYLE TYPE=" style type">...</STYLE>
```

Definition

The <STYLE> tag is currently just a placeholder—it is not commonly used yet. When a standard for style sheets is decided, the <STYLE> tag will be used to implement them.

Category

None

SUB

Compliance

Syntax

```
<SUB>...</SUB>
```

Definition

The `<SUB>` tag displays its contents as subscript—slightly lower than the normal text. Some browsers select the next smaller font size to display the subscript text.

Category

Structural

Example Syntax

```
<SUB>This is subscript text.</SUB>
```

SUP

Compliance

Syntax

```
<SUP>...</SUP>
```

Definition

The ⟨SUP⟩ tag displays its contents as superscript—slightly higher than the normal text. Some browsers select the next smaller font size to display the superscript text.

Category

Structural Definition

Example Syntax

```
<SUP>This is superscript text.</SUP>
```

TAB (not used)

The ⟨TAB⟩ tag was intended to allow tab stops in Web documents. It never made it into the HTML 3.2 standard.

TABLE

Compliance

Syntax

```
<TABLE ALIGN="alignment" BACKGROUND="url of graphic
file"
    BGCOLOR="color" BORDER="numPixels"
    BORDERDARK="color" BORDERLIGHT="color"
    CELLPADDING="numPixels" CELLSPACING="numPixels"
    WIDTH="values">...</TABLE>
```

Definition

The ⟨TABLE⟩ tag defines one or more rows of cells. The attributes of the ⟨TABLE⟩ tag are:

- ALIGN - The `ALIGN` attribute controls the horizontal alignment of the table. Valid values are LEFT, CENTER, and RIGHT.
- BACKGROUND - The Internet Explorer-specific `BACKGROUND` attribute specifies a graphics file to be tiled behind all other text and graphics in a table.
- BGCOLOR - The `BGCOLOR` attribute, while not part of the HTML 3.2 specification, is supported by both Netscape Navigator and Internet Explorer. You can use `BGCOLOR` to set the background color for the table.
- BORDER - The `BORDER` attribute controls the width of the table border in pixels. By setting it to zero, you can use tables to easily align Web page elements.
- BORDERDARK - The Internet Explorer-specific `BORDERDARK` attribute controls the color of the dark side of a 3-D border.
- BORDERLIGHT - The Internet Explorer-specific `BORDERLIGHT` attribute controls the color of the light side of a 3-D border.
- CELLPADDING - The `CELLPADDING` controls the amount of extra space around a cell's contents. If the `CELLPADDING` is zero, cell content is only one pixel away from the cell border. I find most tables are more esthetic when `CELLPADDING` is five pixels.
- CELLSPACING - The `CELLSPACING` attribute controls the width of cell borders displayed in tables.
- WIDTH - The `WIDTH` attribute controls the table's width. You can specify either a specific number of pixels or a percentage. Usually it's a better idea to specify a percentage because of differing monitor sizes and graphic resolutions.

The `<TABLE>` tag can contain one `<CAPTION>` tag and as many `<TH>` and `<TR>` tags as needed. The `<TH>` and `<TR>` tags define the table's rows. The `<TH>` tag is for creating the header row—the cell contents are usually displayed in bold and centered.

NOTE Cox Communications has created a nice tutorial site for HTML tables at **http://www.phx.cox.com/Trial/faq/webfaqs/table/**.

Category

Tables

Example Syntax

```
<!-- The table in this example looks like this:

************************************************************
*             *      A Two Cell Row        *
*             ***************************************
*             * The Left Column * The Right Column *
* A Four Cell Row ***************************
*             * top left cell  * top right cell  *
*             ***************************************
*             * bottom left cell* bottom right cell*
************************************************************
-->
<TABLE BORDER=5 CELLPADDING=5>
 <CAPTION>A Sample Table</CAPTION>
 <TR>
  <TH ROWSPAN=4>A Four Row Cell</TH>
  <TH COLSPAN=2>A Two Column Cell</TH>
 </TR>
 <TR>
  <TH>The left column</TH>
  <TH>The right column</TH>
 </TR>
 <TR>
  <TD>top left cell</TD>
  <TD>top right cell</TD>
 </TR>
 <TR>
  <TD>bottom left cell</TD>
  <TD>bottom right cell</TD>
 </TR>
</TABLE>
```

Related Elements

You can add captions to your table with the <CAPTION> tag. Table rows are defined using the <TH> and <TR> tag. Table cells are defined using the <TD> tag.

TBODY (not used)

The `<TBODY>` tag was intended to group table rows. It never made it into the HTML 3.2 standard.

TD

Compliance

Syntax

```
<TD ALIGN="alignment" COLSPAN="value"
  HEIGHT="numPixels" NOWRAP ROWSPAN="value"
  VALIGN="alignment" WIDTH="numPixels">...</TD>
```

Definition

The `<TD>` tag defines a table cell. It must be contained inside a `<TR>` tag. The attributes of the `<TD>` tag are

- ALIGN - The ALIGN attribute controls the horizontal alignment of the cell's contents. Valid values are LEFT, CENTER, and RIGHT.

- COLSPAN - The COLSPAN attribute controls how many columns the current cell uses. Normally, cells default to a single column.

- HEIGHT - The HEIGHT attribute is used to suggest a height, in pixels, for the cell.

- NOWRAP - The NOWRAP attribute, when present, displays the cell contents as a single line. The `<BR>` tag is used to force line breaks as needed.

- ROWSPAN - The ROWSPAN attribute controls how many rows the current cell uses. Normally, cells default to a single row.

- VALIGN - The VALIGN attribute controls the vertical alignment of the cell's contents. Valid values are TOP, MIDDLE, BOTTOM, and BASELINE.

- WIDTH - The `WIDTH` attribute is used to suggest a width, in pixels, for the cell.

Category

Tables

Example Syntax

```
<!-- The table in this example looks like this:

****************************************************************
*           *       A Two Cell Row       *
*           *************************************
*           * The Left Column * The Right Column *
* A Four Cell Row ****************************
*           * top left cell  * top right cell  *
*           *************************************
*           * bottom left cell* bottom right cell*
****************************************************************
-->
<TABLE BORDER=5 CELLPADDING=5>
 <CAPTION>A Sample Table</CAPTION>
 <TR>
  <TH ROWSPAN=4>A Four Row Cell</TH>
  <TH COLSPAN=2>A Two Column Cell</TH>
 </TR>
 <TR>
  <TH>The left column</TH>
  <TH>The right column</TH>
 </TR>
 <TR>
  <TD>top left cell</TD>
  <TD>top right cell</TD>
 </TR>
 <TR>
  <TD>bottom left cell</TD>
  <TD>bottom right cell</TD>
 </TR>
</TABLE>
```

TEXT (attribute)

Compliance

Syntax

```
<BODY BACKGROUND=" url of graphic file "
   BGPROPERTIES="fixed"
   TEXT=" color"
   LINK=" color" ALINK=" color" VLINK=" color">...</
BODY>
```

Definition

The <TEXT> attribute of the <BODY> tag controls the color of the page's text.

Category

Presentation

Example Syntax

```
<BODY TEXT=RED>This text will be displayed in
red!</BODY>
```

TEXTAREA

Compliance

Syntax

```
<TEXTAREA COLS=" numCols" NAME=" name"
ROWS="numRows">...</TEXTAREA>
```

Definition

The <TEXTAREA> tag creates a multiline input field in a form. The contents of the tag become the default text displays in the input field. The attributes of the <TEXTAREA> tag are

- COLS - The COLS attribute controls the width, in characters, of the input field.
- NAME - The NAME attribute is required and is associated with the value of the input field when the form data is sent to the Web server.
- ROWS - The ROWS attribute controls the height, in characters, of the input field.

Category

Forms

Example Syntax

```
<FORM ACTION="http://www.foo.com/cgi-bin/
register.cgi"
  ENCTYPE="application/x-www-form-urlencoded">
 Enter Name:
 <INPUT TYPE="text" VALUE="David" NAME="First"
SIZE=15>
 <INPUT TYPE="text" VALUE="Medinets" NAME="Last"
SIZE=20>
 <TEXTAREA COLS=25 NAME="Address" ROWS=5>
 <INPUT TYPE="submit">
</FORM>
```

TFOOT (not used)

The <TFOOT> tag was intended to group table rows. It never made it into the HTML 3.2 standard.

TH

Compliance

Syntax

```
<TH ALIGN="alignment" COLSPAN="value"
  HEIGHT="numPixels" NOWRAP ROWSPAN="value"
  VALIGN="alignment" WIDTH="numPixels">...</TD>
```

Definition

The `<TH>` tag defines a table header cell. It must be contained inside a `<TR>` tag. Unlike the `<TD>` tag, the cell contents will be centered and bold. You can use the `<TH>` cells anywhere in a table. However, the tag is intended to represent column heading information.

For long tables, many Webmasters repeat the heading row every five to ten rows so that the column headings are always in view.

The attributes of the `<TH>` tag are

- ALIGN - The `ALIGN` attribute controls the horizontal alignment of the cell's contents. Valid values are LEFT, CENTER, and RIGHT.

- COLSPAN - The `COLSPAN` attribute controls how many columns the current cell uses. Normally, cells default to a single column.

- HEIGHT - The `HEIGHT` attribute is used to suggest a height, in pixels, for the cell.

- NOWRAP - The `NOWRAP` attribute, when present, displays the cell contents as a single line. The `<BR>` tag is used to force line breaks as needed.

- ROWSPAN - The `ROWSPAN` attribute controls how many rows the current cell uses. Normally, cells default to a single row.

- VALIGN - The `VALIGN` attribute controls the vertical alignment of the cell's contents. Valid values are TOP, MIDDLE, BOTTOM, and BASELINE.

- WIDTH - The `WIDTH` attribute is used to suggest a width, in pixels, for the cell.

Category

Tables

Example Syntax

```
<!-- The table in this example looks like this:

*************************************************************
*            *       A Two Cell Row       *
*            **********************************
*            * The Left Column * The Right Column *
* A Four Cell Row   ****************************
*            * top left cell  * top right cell  *
*            **********************************
*            * bottom left cell* bottom right cell*
*************************************************************
-->
<TABLE BORDER=5 CELLPADDING=5>
 <CAPTION>A Sample Table</CAPTION>
 <TR>
  <TH ROWSPAN=4>A Four Row Cell</ TH>
  <TH COLSPAN=2>A Two Column Cell</ TH>
 </TR>
 <TR>
  <TH>The left column</ TH>
  <TH>The right column</ TH>
 </TR>
 <TR>
  <TD>top left cell</TD>
  <TD>top right cell</TD>
 </TR>
 <TR>
  <TD>bottom left cell</TD>
  <TD>bottom right cell</TD>
 </TR>
</TABLE>
```

THEAD (not used)

The `<THEAD>` tag was intended to group table rows. It never made it into the HTML 3.2 standard.

TITLE

Compliance

Syntax

`<TITLE>...</TITLE>`

Definition

The `<TITLE>` tag specifies the title of the Web page. It must be contained inside the `<HEAD>` tag. The Web page title is very important. It should concisely describe the content and intent of the page.

Category

Structural

Example Syntax

```
<HEAD>
 <TITLE>CodeBits' Home Page</TITLE>
</HEAD>
```

TR

Compliance

Syntax

`<TR ALIGN="alignment" VALIGN="alignement">...</TR>`

Definition

The `<TR>` tag defines a row in a table. It acts as a container for `<TH>` and `<TD>` tags. The attributes of the `<TR>` tag are

- ALIGN - The ALIGN attribute controls the default horizontal alignment of the cell contents. Valid values are LEFT, CENTER, and RIGHT.
- VALIGN - The VALIGN attribute controls the default vertical alignment of the cell contents. Valid values are TOP, MIDDLE, BOTTOM, and BASELINE.

Category

Tables

Example Syntax

```
<!-- The table in this example looks like this:

************************************************************
*            *       A Two Cell Row           *
*            *****************************************
*            * The Left Column * The Right Column *
* A Four Cell Row  *****************************************
*            * top left cell  * top right cell   *
*            *****************************************
*            * bottom left cell* bottom right cell*
************************************************************
```

```
-->
<TABLE BORDER=5 CELLPADDING=5>
 <CAPTION>A Sample Table</CAPTION>
 <TR>
  <TH ROWSPAN=4>A Four Row Cell</TH>
  <TH COLSPAN=2>A Two Column Cell</TH>
 </TR>
 <TR>
  <TH>The left column</TH>
  <TH>The right column</TH>
 </TR>
 <TR>
  <TD>top left cell</TD>
  <TD>top right cell</TD>
 </TR>
 <TR>
  <TD>bottom left cell</TD>
  <TD>bottom right cell</TD>
 </TR>
</TABLE>
```

TT

Compliance

Syntax

<TT>...</TT>

Definition

The <TT> tag displays its contents in a fixed-width font. Text inside the <TT> tag has multiple spaces collapsed into one and all new lines are ignored.

Category

Presentation

Example Syntax

```
<P>Sometimes the only answer is using
a <TT>fixed width</TT> font.</P>
```

Related Elements

If possible, use the `<CODE>`, `<KBD>`, or `<SAMP>` tags. They will convey the intent of the text better. For multiple lines of fixed-width font, use the PRE tag.

U

Compliance

Syntax

```
<U>...</U>
```

Definition

The `<U>` tag displays its contents with an underline.

Category

Structural

Example Syntax

```
<U>This text will be underlined!</U>
```

UL

Compliance

Syntax

```
<UL COMPACT TYPE="options">...</UL>
```

Definition

The `<UL>` tag indicates the beginning of an unordered or bulleted list. The attributes of the `<UL>` tag are

- COMPACT - The COMPACT attribute directs the browser to minimize spaces between individual items in a list. It does not seem to change the display in Netscape Navigator or Internet Explorer Web browsers.
- TYPE - The TYPE attribute controls which bullet is used to start the list. Valid values are DISC, SQUARE, and CIRCLE.

Category

Lists

Example Syntax

```
<UL>
 <LI>The first item
 <LI>The second item
</UL>
```

USEMAP (attribute)

Compliance

Syntax

```
<IMG ALIGN="alignment" ALT="alternative text"
   BORDER="numPixels" CONTROLS DYNSRC="animation
file"
   HEIGHT="numPixels" HSPACE="numPixels" ISMAP
LOOP="options"
   SRC="url of image file" USEMAP="url of map"
   VSPACE="numPixels" WIDTH="numPixels">
```

Definition

The USEMAP attribute of the <IMG> tag indicates the image is a client-side image map. An example of client-side image maps is shown in the entry for the <MAP> tag.

Category

Graphics, Links

Example Syntax

You can see the following example in action at **http://www.purplecanyon.com**. Notice that comments are used to document the <MAP> tag.

```
<MAP NAME="menu">
 <!-- #$AUTHOR:Purple Canyon Web Designs -->
 <!-- #$DATE:Mon Jan 06 05:55:25 1997 -->
 <!-- #$PATH:C:\web projects\Web
Projects\purplecanyon\images\ -->
 <!-- #$GIF:rocks_h.jpg -->
 <AREA SHAPE=CIRCLE COORDS="63,48,49"
HREF="graphix.html">
```

```
 <AREA SHAPE=CIRCLE COORDS="133,126,48"
HREF="why.html">
 <AREA SHAPE=CIRCLE COORDS="228,105,44"
HREF="clients.html">
 <AREA SHAPE=RECT COORDS="134,182,239,249"
HREF="prices.html">
 <AREA SHAPE=POLY
COORDS="10,148,23,227,111,203,45,123,10,148"
   HREF="contact.html">
 <AREA SHAPE=default HREF="http://
www.purplecanyon.com">
</MAP>
<img src="images/rocks_h.jpg" width=265 height=261
  border=0 alt="Choose!!!!!" usemap=#menu>
```

VAR

Compliance

Syntax

```
<VAR>...</VAR>
```

Definition

The `<VAR>` tag is used to represent a variable in a computer program. The actual display of the text varies from browser to browser.

Category

Structural

Example Syntax

```
<P>In that last example, <VAR>numBooks</VAR> was
used to represent the number of books.</P>
```

VLINK (attribute)

Compliance

Syntax

```
<BODY BACKGROUND=" url of graphic file "
   BGPROPERTIES="fixed"
   TEXT=" color"
   LINK=" color" ALINK=" color" VLINK=" color">...</
BODY>
```

Definition

The VLINK attribute of the <BODY> tag controls the color of the visited hyperlinked text on the page.

Category

Links

Example Syntax

```
<BODY VLINK="green">Visited shortcuts will be
green!</BODY>
```

VSPACE (attribute)

Compliance

Syntax

```
<IMG ALIGN="alignment" ALT="alternative text"
   BORDER="numPixels" CONTROLS DYNSRC="animation
file"
   HEIGHT="numPixels" HSPACE="numPixels" ISMAP
LOOP="options"
   SRC="url of image file" USEMAP="url of map"
   VSPACE="numPixels" WIDTH="numPixels">

<MARQUEE ALIGN="alignment" BEHAVIOR="options"
     BGCOLOR="color" DIRECTION="direction"
     HEIGHT="value" HSPACE="numPixels"
     LOOP="options" SCROLLAMOUNT="numPixels"
     SCROLLDELAY="numMilliseconds"
     VSPACE="numPixels"
     WIDTH="numPixels">...</MARQUEE>
```

Definition

The VSPACE attribute of the <IMG> and <MARQUEE> tags controls the amount of blank space that buffers the image from other elements on the top and bottom sides of the marquee.

Category

None

Example Syntax

```
<IMG BORDER=0 HEIGHT=153 SRC="logo.gif" WIDTH=575
VSPACE=10>
```

WBR (obsolete)

The <WBR> tag was used to force line breaks inside the <NOBR> tag. However, because the <NOBR> tag was superseded by the <PRE> tag, <WBR> is no longer needed.

HTML REFERENCE TABLES

HTML Characters from ISO 8859-1

Binary	Text	Description	Displays
"	"	Double quote	"
&	&	Ampersand	&
<	<	Less than	<
>	>	Greater than	>
		Non-breaking space	
¡	¡	Inverted exclamation point	¡
¢	¢	Cent sign	¢
£	£	Pound sign	£
¤	¤	General currency sign	¤
¥	¥	Yen sign	¥
¦	¦	Broken (vertical) bar	¦
§	§	Section sign	§
¨	¨	Umlaut/dieresis	¨
©	©	Copyright sign	©
ª	ª	Ordinal indicator, fem	ª
«	«	Angle quotation mark, left	«
¬	¬	Not sign	¬
­	­	Soft hyphen	-
®	®	Registered sign	®
¯	¯	Macron	‾

continues

HTML Reference Tables

continued

Binary	Text	Description	Displays
°	°	Degree sign	°
±	±	Plus over minus sign	±
²	²	Superscript two	²
³	³	Superscript three	³
´	´	Acute accent	´
µ	µ	Micro sign	µ
¶	¶	Pilcrow (paragraph sign)	¶
·	·	Middle dot	·
¸	¸	Cedilla	¸
¹	¹	Superscript one	¹
º	º	Ordinal indicator, male	º
»	»	Angle quotation mark, right	»
¼	¼	Fraction one-quarter	¼
½	½	Fraction one-half	½
¾	¾	Fraction three-quarters	¾
;¿	¿	Inverted question mark	¿
À	À	A grave	À
Á	Á	A acute	Á
Â	Â	A circumflex	Â
Ã	Ã	A tilde	Ã
Ä	Ä	A umlaut	Ä
Å	Å	A ring	Å
Æ	&Aelig;	AE ligature	Æ
Ç	Ç	C cedilla	Ç
È	È	E grave	È
É	É	E acute	É
Ê	Ê	E circumflex	Ê

HTML Characters from ISO 8859-1

Binary	Text	Description	Displays
Ë	Ë	E umlaut	Ë
Ì	Ì	I grave	Ì
Í	Í	I acute	Í
Î	Î	I circumflex	Î
Ï	Ï	I umlaut	Ï
Ð	Ð	ETH	Ð
Ñ	Ñ	N tilde	Ñ
Ò	Ò	O grave	Ò
Ó	Ó	O acute	Ó
Ô	Ô	O circumflex	Ô
Õ	Õ	O tilde	Õ
Ö	Ö	O umlaut	Ö
×	×	Multiply sign	×
Ø	Ø	O slash	Ø
Ù	Ù	U grave	Ù
Ú	Ú	U acute	Ú
Û	Û	U circumflex	Û
Ü	Ü	U umlaut	Ü
Ý	Ý	Y acute	Ý
Þ	Þ	THORN	Þ
ß	ß	sharp s	β
à	à	a grave	à
á	á	a acute	á
â	â	a circumflex	â
ã	ã	a tilde	ã
ä	ä	a umlaut	ä
å	å	a ring	å

continues

HTML Reference Tables

continued

Binary	Text	Description	Displays
æ	æ	ae ligature	æ
ç	ç	c cedilla	ç
è	è	e grave	è
é	é	e acute	é
ê	ê	e circumflex	ê
ë	ë	e umlaut	ë
ì	ì	i grave	ì
í	í	i acute	í
î	î	i circumflex	î
ï	ï	I umlaut	ï
ð	ð	eth	ð
ñ	ñ	n tilde	ñ
ò	ò	o grave	ò
ó	ó	o acute	ó
ô	ô	o circumflex	ô
õ	õ	o tilde	õ
ö	ö	o umlaut	ö
÷	÷	Division sign	÷
ø	ø	o slash	ø
ù	ù	u grave	ù
ú	ú	u acute	ú
û	û	u circumflex	û
ü	ü	u umlaut	ü
ý	ý	y acute	ý
þ	þ	thorn	þ
ÿ	ÿ	y umlaut	ÿ

Color Tables

These two color tables will help you find a color name by referencing the Hex/RGB value or find the Hex/RGB value when you reference the color name.

Proposed Color Codes Sorted by Color Name		Proposed Color Codes Sorted by Value	
Find the Color Name	**Look Up the Value Here**	**Find the Value Here**	**Look Up the Color Name Here**
White	rgb=#FFFFFF	rgb=#000000	Black
Red	rgb=#FF0000	rgb=#00009C	New Midnight Blue
Green	rgb=#00FF00	rgb=#0000FF	Blue
Blue	rgb=#0000FF	rgb=#007FFF	Slate Blue
Magenta	rgb=#FF00FF	rgb=#00FF00	Green
Cyan	rgb=#00FFFF	rgb=#00FF7F	Spring Green
Yellow	rgb=#FFFF00	rgb=#00FFFF	Cyan
Black	rgb=#000000	rgb=#215E21	Hunter Green
Aquamarine	rgb=#70DB93	rgb=#23238E	Navy Blue
Baker's Chocolate	rgb=#5C3317	rgb=#236B8E	Steel Blue
Blue Violet	rgb=#9F5F9F	rgb=#238E23	Forest Green
Brass	rgb=#B5A642	rgb=#238E68	Sea Green
Bright Gold	rgb=#D9D919	rgb=#2F2F4F	Midnight Blue
Brown	rgb=#A62A2A	rgb=#2F4F2F	Dark Green
Bronze	rgb=#8C7853	rgb=#2F4F4F	Dark Slate Gray
Bronze II	rgb=#A67D3D	rgb=#3232CD	Medium Blue
Cadet Blue	rgb=#5F9F9F	rgb=#3299CC	Sky Blue
Cool Copper	rgb=#D98719	rgb=#32CD32	Lime Green
Copper	rgb=#B87333	rgb=#32CD99	Medium Aquamarine

continues

HTML Reference Tables

continued

Proposed Color Codes Sorted by Color Name		Proposed Color Codes Sorted by Value	
Find the Color Name	**Look Up the Value Here**	**Find the Value Here**	**Look Up the Color Name Here**
Coral	rgb=#FF7F00	rgb=#38B0DE	Summer Sky
Cornflower Blue	rgb=#42426F	rgb=#42426F	Cornflower Blue
Dark Brown	rgb=#5C4033	rgb=#426F42	Medium Sea Green
Dark Green	rgb=#2F4F2F	rgb=#4A766E	Dark Green Copper
Dark Green Copper	rgb=#4A766E	rgb=#4D4DFF	Neon Blue
Dark Olive Green	rgb=#4F4F2F	rgb=#4E2F2F	Indian Red
Dark Orchid	rgb=#9932CD	rgb=#4F2F4F	Violet
Dark Purple	rgb=#871F78	rgb=#4F4F2F	Dark Olive Green
Dark Slate Blue	rgb=#6B238E	rgb=#527F76	Green Copper
Dark Slate Gray	rgb=#2F4F4F	rgb=#545454	Dim Gray
Dark Tan	rgb=#97694F	rgb=#5959AB	Rich Blue
Dark Turquoise	rgb=#7093DB	rgb=#5C3317	Baker's Chocolate
Dark Wood	rgb=#855E42	rgb=#5C4033	Dark Brown
Dim Gray	rgb=#545454	rgb=#5C4033	Very Dark Brown
Dusty Rose	rgb=#856363	rgb=#5F9F9F	Cadet Blue
Feldspar	rgb=#D19275	rgb=#6B238E	Dark Slate Blue
Firebrick	rgb=#8E2323	rgb=#6B4226	Semi-Sweet Chocolate
Forest Green	rgb=#238E23	rgb=#6B8E23	Medium Forest Green
Gold	rgb=#CD7F32	rgb=#6F4242	Salmon
Goldenrod	rgb=#DBDB70	rgb=#7093DB	Dark Turquoise
Gray	rgb=#C0C0C0	rgb=#70DB93	Aquamarine
Green Copper	rgb=#527F76	rgb=#70DBDB	Medium Turquoise
Green Yellow	rgb=#93DB70	rgb=#7F00FF	Medium Slate Blue

Color Tables

Proposed Color Codes Sorted by Color Name

Find the Color Name	Look Up the Value Here
Hunter Green	rgb=#215E21
Indian Red	rgb=#4E2F2F
Khaki	rgb=#9F9F5F
Light Blue	rgb=#C0D9D9
Light Gray	rgb=#A8A8A8
Light Steel Blue	rgb=#8F8FBD
Light Wood	rgb=#E9C2A6
Lime Green	rgb=#32CD32
Mandarin Orange	rgb=#E47833
Maroon	rgb=#8E236B
Medium Aquamarine	rgb=#32CD99
Medium Blue	rgb=#3232CD
Medium Forest Green	rgb=#6B8E23
Medium Goldenrod	rgb=#EAEAAE
Medium Orchid	rgb=#9370DB
Medium Sea Green	rgb=#426F42
Medium Slate Blue	rgb=#7F00FF
Medium Spring Green	rgb=#7FFF00
Medium Turquoise	rgb=#70DBDB
Medium Violet Red	rgb=#DB7093
Medium Wood	rgb=#A68064

Proposed Color Codes Sorted by Value

Find the Value Here	Look Up the Color Name Here
rgb=#7FFF00	Medium Spring Green
rgb=#855E42	Dark Wood
rgb=#856363	Dusty Rose
rgb=#871F78	Dark Purple
rgb=#8C1717	Scarlet
rgb=#8C7853	Bronze
rgb=#8E2323	Firebrick
rgb=#8E236B	Maroon
rgb=#8E6B23	Sienna
rgb=#8F8FBD	Light Steel Blue
rgb=#8FBC8F	Pale Green
rgb=#9370DB	Medium Orchid
rgb=#93DB70	Green Yellow
rgb=#97694F	Dark Tan
rgb=#9932CD	Dark Orchid
rgb=#99CC32	Yellow Green
rgb=#9F5F9F	Blue Violet
rgb=#9F9F5F	Khaki
rgb=#A62A2A	Brown
rgb=#A67D3D	Bronze II
rgb=#A68064	Medium Wood

continues

HTML Reference Tables

continued

Proposed Color Codes Sorted by Color Name		Proposed Color Codes Sorted by Value	
Find the Color Name	**Look Up the Value Here**	**Find the Value Here**	**Look Up the Color Name Here**
Midnight Blue	rgb=#2F2F4F	rgb=#A8A8A8	Light Gray
Navy Blue	rgb=#23238E	rgb=#ADEAEA	Turquoise
Neon Blue	rgb=#4D4DFF	rgb=#B5A642	Brass
Neon Pink	rgb=#FF6EC7	rgb=#B87333	Copper
New Midnight Blue	rgb=#00009C	rgb=#BC8F8F	Pink
New Tan	rgb=#EBC79E	rgb=#C0C0C0	Gray
Old Gold	rgb=#CFB53B	rgb=#C0D9D9	Light Blue
Orange	rgb=#FF7F00	rgb=#CC3299	Violet Red
Orange Red	rgb=#FF2400	rgb=#CD7F32	Gold
Orchid	rgb=#DB70DB	rgb=#CDCDCD	Very Light Gray
Pale Green	rgb=#8FBC8F	rgb=#CFB53B	Old Gold
Pink	rgb=#BC8F8F	rgb=#D19275	Feldspar
Plum	rgb=#EAADEA	rgb=#D8BFD8	Thistle
Quartz	rgb=#D9D9F3	rgb=#D8D8BF	Wheat
Rich Blue	rgb=#5959AB	rgb=#D98719	Cool Copper
Salmon	rgb=#6F4242	rgb=#D9D919	Bright Gold
Scarlet	rgb=#8C1717	rgb=#D9D9F3	Quartz
Sea Green	rgb=#238E68	rgb=#DB7093	Medium Violet Red
Semi-Sweet Choc.	rgb=#6B4226	rgb=#DB70DB	Orchid
Sienna	rgb=#8E6B23	rgb=#DB9370	Tan
Silver	rgb=#E6E8FA	rgb=#DBDB70	Goldenrod
Sky Blue	rgb=#3299CC	rgb=#E47833	Mandarin Orange
Slate Blue	rgb=#007FFF	rgb=#E6E8FA	Silver
Spicy Pink	rgb=#FF1CAE	rgb=#E9C2A6	Light Wood

Proposed Color Codes Sorted by Color Name		Proposed Color Codes Sorted by Value	
Find the Color Name	Look Up the Value Here	Find the Value Here	Look Up the Color Name Here
Spring Green	rgb=#00FF7F	rgb=#EAADEA	Plum
Steel Blue	rgb=#236B8E	rgb=#EAEAAE	Medium Goldenrod
Summer Sky	rgb=#38B0DE	rgb=#EBC79E	New Tan
Tan	rgb=#DB9370	rgb=#FF0000	Red
Thistle	rgb=#D8BFD8	rgb=#FF00FF	Magenta
Turquoise	rgb=#ADEAEA	rgb=#FF1CAE	Spicy Pink
Very Dark Brown	rgb=#5C4033	rgb=#FF2400	Orange Red
Very Light Gray	rgb=#CDCDCD	rgb=#FF6EC7	Neon Pink
Violet	rgb=#4F2F4F	rgb=#FF7F00	Coral
Violet Red	rgb=#CC3299	rgb=#FF7F00	Orange
Wheat	rgb=#D8D8BF	rgb=#FFFF00	Yellow
Yellow Green	rgb=#99CC32	rgb=#FFFFFF	White

Newsgroups for HTML Authors and Web Professionals

This table is a source of various newsgroups focusing on Internet-related topics of interest to many HTML authors and Web site administrators. The column on the left of this table contains special-interest newsgroup addresses. The column to the right is a description of each newsgroup.

Browsers and Servers	Description
comp.infosystems.www.browsers.ms-windows	Web browsers for Windows 3.1 and Windows 95

continues

HTML Reference Tables

continued

Browsers and Servers	Description
comp.infosystems.www.servers.ms-windows	Web servers for Windows 95 and NT Web Content Development
comp.infosystems.www.authoring.cgi	Authoring CGI scripts
comp.infosystems.www.authoring.html	Authoring HTML
comp.infosystems.www.authoring.images	Using Images
comp.infosystems.www.authoring.misc	Web authoring issues, Internet technologies, and Windows
alt.lang.basic	The BASIC programming language
alt.lang.vrml	VRML
alt.winsock	Windows Sockets, general languages, tools
alt.winsock.programming	Windows Sockets programming
alt.winsock.voice	Voice-data
comp.lang.basic	More on the BASIC language
comp.lang.basic.misc	Yet more coverage of the BASIC language
comp.lang.basic.visual.3rdparty	Visual Basic 3-D add-ins
comp.lang.basic.visual.database	Database aspects of Visual Basic
comp.lang.c	Topic: The C programming language
comp.lang.c++	Topic: The C++ programming language
comp.os.ms-windows.apps.winsock.mail	Windows Sockets and e-mail
comp.os.ms-windows.apps.winsock.misc	Other Windows Sockets issues
comp.os.ms-windows.apps.winsock.news	Windows Sockets and news apps
comp.os.ms-windows.networking.misc	More networking
comp.os.ms-windows.networking.tcp-ip	TCP/IP
comp.os.ms-windows.networking.win95	Windows 95

Newsgroups for HTML Authors and Web Professionals

Browsers and Servers	Description
comp.os.ms-windows.programmer.controls	Controls, objects, and VBXs
comp.os.ms-windows.programmer.tools.winsock	Windows Sockets programming
comp.os.ms-windows.programmer.tools.winsock	Windows Sockets programming tools
Tools and Technologies for the Enterprise	
comp.databases.ms-access	Microsoft Access
comp.databases.ms-sqlserver	Microsoft SQL Server
comp.os.ms-windows.nt.software.backoffice	Microsoft Windows NT/BackOffice
Data Security, Data Encryption	
comp.security.misc	Security issues
sci.crypt	Topic: Cryptography
technologiescomp.security.announce	Announcements in security technology

GLOSSARY

The Internet can be rather confusing to new users. It has its own jargon, just as many professions or hobbies do. Learning the jargon can make the Internet less foreign to you. As the Internet grows over the years, a whole vocabulary is developing to describe Internet features and related activities. As you read documents and participate in conversations on the Internet, you may come across terms that you are unfamiliar with. This section explains some of the most common terms you may encounter.

account   A user ID and disk area restricted for the use of a particular person. Usually password protected.

ACM   Association for Computing Machinery, a professional society for people connected with the computer industry.

address   See e-mail address and host address.

Agent   The commercial version of the Free Agent news reader.

alias   A short name used to represent a more complicated one. Often used for mail addresses or host domain names.

America Online   A commercial online service (normally abbreviated as AOL) that gives its subscribers access to the Internet in addition to its other features.

analog   A form of electronic communication using a continuous electromagnetic wave, such as television or radio. Any continuous wave form, as opposed to digital on/off transmissions.

Archie   An application that allows you to search easily for information at anonymous FTP sites on the Internet.

archive   A repository of files available for access at an Internet site. Also, a collection of files—often a backup of a disk, or files saved to tape to allow them to be transferred.

ARPA   (Advanced Research Projects Agency) A government agency that originally funded the research on the ARPANET (became DARPA in the mid 1970s).

ARPANET   An experimental communications network funded by the government that eventually developed into the Internet.

article   Message submitted to a UseNet newsgroup. Unlike an e-mail message that goes to a specific person or group of persons, a newsgroup message goes to directories (on many machines) that can be read by any number of people.

ASCII   Data that is limited to letters, numbers, and punctuation. ASCII stands for American Standard Code for Information Interchange.

ATM   (Asynchronous Transfer Mode) A developing technological advance in communications switching. This technology uses hardware switches to create a temporary direct path between two destinations so data can be exchanged at a higher rate.

attribute   A form of a "command line switch" as applied to tags in the HTML language. HTML commands or "tags" can be more specific when attributes are used. Not all HTML tags utilize attributes.

AUP   (Acceptable Use Policy) The restrictions that a network segment places on the traffic it carries. (These policies were more prevalent when the government was running the Internet backbone.)

backbone   The major communications lines of a network.

bandwidth   The maximum volume of data that can be sent over a communications network.

bang   A slang term for an exclamation point.

bang address   A type of e-mail address that separates host names in the address with exclamation points. Used for mail sent to the UUCP network, where specifying the exact path of the mail (including all hosts that pass on the message) is necessary. The address is in the form of machine!machine!userID, where the number of machines listed depends on the connections needed to reach the machine where the account userID is.

BBS   (Bulletin Board System) A system that allows you to connect to a computer to upload and download files and leave messages for other users.

binary   Data that may contain non-printable characters, including graphics files, programs, sound files, and ZIP (compressed file) archives.

BinHex   A program, predominantly used on the Macintosh, that is used to encode binary files as ASCII so that they can be sent through e-mail. BinHex is a data format used for the encoding, as well as being the name of the program.

bit   The basic unit of digital communications. There are eight bits in a byte.

BITNET   (Because It's Time Network) A non-TCP/IP network for small universities without Internet access.

bookmarks   Term used by some World Wide Web browsers for saving URLs that you access frequently. Microsoft uses the term "Favorite Places" instead of bookmark.

bot (IRC)   A program that watches an IRC channel and automatically responds when certain messages are entered.

bounce   An e-mail message you receive that tells you that an e-mail message you sent wasn't delivered. Usually contains an error code and the contents of the message that weren't delivered.

bps   (bits per second) Units of measure that express the speed at which data is transferred between computers.

bridge   A device that connects one physical section of a network to another, often providing isolation.

browser   A utility that lets you look through collections of things. For example, a file browser lets you look through a file system. Applications that let you access the World Wide Web are called Web browsers.

BTW   (by the way) An abbreviation often used in online conversations.

byte   A digital storage unit large enough to contain one ASCII character. Compare to bit.

CERN   The European Laboratory for Particle Physics, where the World Wide Web was first conceived of and implemented.

channel   An Internet Relay Chat term that refers to a group of people discussing a particular topic.

CIX   (Commercial Internet Exchange) A consortium of commercial providers of Internet service.

client   User of a service. Also often refers to a piece of software that gets information from a server.

CNRI (Corporation for National Research Initiatives) An organization formed to foster research into a national data highway.

coaxial A type of wiring where the signal wire is in the center of a shielded cable. Compare to twisted pair.

command line Line on a terminal-based interface where you enter commands to the operating system. Some Internet accounts (usually called shell accounts) are command-line based.

compress A program that compacts a file so it fits into a smaller space. Also can refer to the technique of reducing the amount of space a file takes up.

CompuServe A commercial on-line service that gives its subscribers access to the Internet in addition to its other features.

CPSR (Computer Professionals for Social Responsibility) An organization that encourages socially responsible use of computers.

CREN (Corporation for Research and Educational Networking) An organization formed by the joining of two different educational networks to enhance the capabilities of the two networks.

CWIS (Campus Wide Information Service) A hypertext-based system that provides information about people and services on a campus.

cyberspace A term used to refer to the entire collection of sites accessible electronically. If your computer is attached to the Internet or another large network, it exists in cyberspace.

daemon A program that runs automatically on a computer to perform a service for the operating system.

DARPA (Defense Advanced Research Projects Agency, originally ARPA) The government agency that funded the research that developed the ARPANET.

dedicated line See leased line.

DES (Data Encryption Standard) An algorithm developed by the U.S. government to provide security for data transmitted over a network.

dialup A type of connection where you use a modem to connect to another computer or an Internet provider via phone lines.

digest A form of mailing list where a number of messages are concatenated (linked) and sent out as a single message.

digital   Type of communication used by computers, consisting of individual on and off pulses.

DNS   See Domain Name System.

DOD   (Department of Defense) A U.S. government agency that originally sponsored the ARPANET research.

domain   Highest subdivision of the Internet, for the most part by country (except in the U.S., where it's by type of organization, such as educational, commercial, and government). Usually the last part of a host name; for example, the domain part of ibm.com is .com, which represents the domain of commercial sites in the U.S.

Domain Name System   (DNS) The system that translates between Internet IP addresses and Internet host names.

dot address   See host address.

download   To move a file from a remote computer to your local computer.

ECPA   (Electronic Communications Privacy Act) A law that governs the use and restrictions of electronic communications.

EDUCOM   A nonprofit consortium of educational institutions that help introduce electronic information access and management into educational organizations.

EFF   (Electronic Frontier Foundation) An organization concerned with the legal rights and responsibilities of computer usage.

e-mail   An electronic message delivered from one computer user to another. Short for electronic mail.

e-mail address   An address used to send e-mail to a user on the Internet, consisting of the user name and host name (and any other necessary information, such as a gateway machine). An Internet e-mail address is usually of the form username@hostname.

emoticon   See smiley face entry. The word "emoticon" comes from "emotion" and "icon."

encryption   The process of using a key to scramble a message so that it can be read only by someone who has the key and knows how to unscramble it.

EtherNet   A type of local area network hardware. Many TCP/IP networks are EtherNet-based.

EUDORA   A popular e-mail application.

expire   Remove an article from a UseNet newsgroup after a specified interval.

extension   An enhancement or addition to an existing HTML standard. Extensions are usually referred to in the context of the HTML language. Netscape and Microsoft utilize extensions to the HTML standards that are proprietary to their own browser products. See browser.

FAQ   (Frequently Asked Question document, often pronounced "fak") Contains a list of commonly asked questions on a topic. Most UseNet newsgroups have a FAQ to introduce new readers to popular topics in the newsgroup.

FARNET   A group of networks interested in promoting research and education networking.

Favorite Places   Term used by Internet Explorer when saving URLs that you access frequently.

feed   Send UseNet newsgroups from your site to another site that wants to read them.

finger   A program that provides information about users on an Internet host (may include a user's personal information, such as project affiliation and schedule).

firewall   A device placed on a network to prevent unauthorized traffic from entering the network.

flame   Communicate in an abusive or absurd manner. Often occurs in newsgroup posts and e-mail messages.

forms   Online data entry sheets supported by some World Wide Web browsers.

frame relay   A type of digital data communications protocol.

Free Agent   A popular freeware news reader.

freeware   Software that is made available by the author at no cost to anyone who wants it (although the author retains rights to the software).

FTP   (File Transfer Protocol) An Internet communications protocol that allows you to transfer files between hosts on the Internet.

FWIW   (For What It's Worth) An abbreviation often used in online conversations.

FYI   (For Your Information) An abbreviation used often in online conversations. An FYI is also a type of Internet reference document that contains answers to basic questions about the Internet.

gateway   A device that interfaces two networks that use different protocols.

gigabit   Very high-speed (1 billion bits per second) data communication.

gigabyte   A unit of data storage approximately equal to 1 billion bytes of data.

Gopher   An application that allows you to access publicly available information on compatible Internet hosts that provide the Gopher service.

Gopherbook   An application that uses an interface resembling a book to access Gopher servers.

GUI   (Graphical User Interface) A computer interface based on graphical symbols rather than text. Windowing environments and Macintosh environments are GUIs.

gzip   A file compression program originally designed to replace the UNIX compression utility.

hacking   Originally referred to playing around with computer systems; now often used to indicate destructive computer activity.

headers   Lines at the beginning of an e-mail message or newsgroup post that contain information about the message: its source, destination, subject, and route it took to get there, among other things.

hop-check   A utility that allows you to find out how many routers are between your host and another Internet host. See also traceroute.

host address   A unique number assigned to identify a host on the Internet (also called IP address or dot address). This address is usually represented as four numbers between 1 and 254 and separated by periods—for example, 192.58.107.230.

host name   A unique name for a host that corresponds to the host address.

hosts   Individual computers connected to the Internet; see also nodes.

HotDog   A popular shareware HTML editor.

HTML   (HyperText Markup Language) The formatting language that is used to create World Wide Web documents.

HTTP   (HyperText Transport Protocol) The communications protocol that allows WWW hypertext documents to be retrieved quickly.

hypertext   A document that has words or graphics containing links to other documents. Usually, selecting the link area on-screen (with a mouse or keyboard command) activates these links.

hypertext links   The areas (words or graphics) in an HTML document that cause another document to be loaded when the user clicks them.

IAB   (Internet Architecture Board) A group of volunteers who work to maintain the Internet.

IEEE   (Institute of Electrical and Electronic Engineers) The professional society for electrical and computer engineers.

IETF   (Internet Engineering Task Force) A group of volunteers that develops Internet standards.

IMHO   (In My Humble—or Honest—Opinion) An abbreviation often used in online conversations.

Internet   The term used to describe all the worldwide interconnected TCP/IP networks.

Internet Assistant   Microsoft applications that allow you to develop HTML documents in many of the Microsoft Office applications.

Internet Explorer   A Microsoft Web browser.

Internet Society   See ISOC.

InterNIC   The NSFNET manager sites on the Internet that provide information about the Internet.

IP   (Internet Protocol) The communications protocol used by computers connected to the Internet.

IP address   See host address.

IRC   (Internet Relay Chat) A live conference facility available on the Internet.

ISDN   (Integrated Services Digital Network) An emerging digital communications standard, allowing faster speeds than are possible using modems over analog phone lines.

ISO   (International Standards Organization) An organization that sets worldwide standards in many different areas. For example, the organization has been working on a network protocol to replace TCP/IP (this isn't widely supported, however).

ISOC   (Internet Society) An educational organization dedicated to encouraging use of the Internet.

kill file   A file used by some news reader software that allows you to automatically skip posts with certain attributes (specific subject, author, and so on).

knowbots   (Knowledge robots) Programs that automatically search through a network for specified information.

labels   The different components of an Internet host name.

LAN   (Local Area Network) A network of computers that is limited to a (usually) small physical area, like a building.

leased line   A dedicated phone line used for network communications.

listproc   Software that automates the management of electronic mailing lists. See also LISTSERV, majordomo, SmartList.

LISTSERV   Software that automates the management of electronic mailing lists. See also listproc, majordomo, SmartList.

local   Pertaining to the computer you are now using.

local host   The computer you are currently using.

login   Provides a user-ID and password to allow you to use the resources of a computer.

lurking   Observing but not participating in an activity, usually a UseNet newsgroup or IRC channel.

mail reflector   Software that automatically distributes all submitted messages to the members of a mailing list.

mailers   Applications that let you read and send e-mail messages.

mailing list   A service that forwards an e-mail message sent to it to everyone on a list, allowing a group of people to discuss a particular topic.

majordomo   Software that automates the management of electronic mailing lists. See also listproc, LISTSERV, SmartList.

man   A UNIX command that provides information about UNIX commands. (man is short for manual entry.)

MBONE   (Multicast backbone) An experimental network that allows live video to be sent over the Internet.

Merit   (Michigan Educational Research Information Triad) The organization that initially managed NSFNET.

MILNET   DOD's (Department of Defense) network.

MIME   (Multipurpose Internet Multimedia Extensions) An extension to Internet mail that allows for the inclusion of nontextual data such as video and audio in e-mail.

modem   An electronic device that allows digital computer data to be transmitted via analog phone lines.

moderator   A person who examines all submissions to a moderated newsgroup or mailing list and allows only those that meet certain criteria to be posted. Usually, the moderator makes sure that the topic is pertinent to the group and that the submissions aren't flames. Most newsgroups are unmoderated.

Mosaic   A graphical interface to the World Wide Web (WWW).

MOTD   (Message of the day) A message posted on some computer systems to let people know about problems or new developments.

MSN   (Microsoft Network) A commercial online service run by Microsoft that allows access to the Internet in addition to its other features.

MUDs   (Multi-User Dungeons) Interactive real-time text-based games accessible to anyone on the Internet.

multimedia   Presenting information using more than one type of media; for example, sound, text, and graphics.

NCSA   (National Center for Supercomputing Applications)   A division of the University of Illinois where the first World Wide Web Browser and HTML standards were developed.

NETCOM NetCruiser   A complete Internet service package.

Netfind   A service that allows you to look up an Internet user's address.

netiquette   Network etiquette conventions used in written communication, usually referring to UseNet newsgroup postings, but also applicable to e-mail and IRC discussions.

NetManage   The producer of Chameleon, a popular TCP/IP package that provides interfaces to a number of Internet services for Windows.

netnews   A collective way of referring to the UseNet newsgroups.

NetScape Navigator   A popular commercial World Wide Web browser.

network   A number of computers physically connected to enable communication with one another.

news readers   Applications that let you read (and usually post) articles in UseNet newsgroups.

newsgroups   The electronic discussion groups of UseNet.

NFS   (Network File System) A file system developed by Sun Microsystems that is now widely used on many different networks.

NIC   (Network Information Center) A service that provides administrative information about a network.

NII   (National Information Infrastructure) The government's vision of a high-speed network giving everyone in the country access to advanced computer capabilities.

NNTP   (Network News Transport Protocol) The communications protocol that is used to send UseNet news on the Internet.

nodes   Individual computers connected to a network; see also hosts.

NREN   (National Research and Education Network) A proposed nation-wide high-speed data network to be used for educational and research purposes.

NSF   (National Science Foundation) Current supporter of the main Internet backbone in the U.S.

NSFNET   Network funded by the National Science Foundation, now the backbone of the Internet.

OC3   (Optical Carrier 3) A protocol for communications over a high-speed optical network.

online   Existing in electronic form (e.g., online documentation). Also, connected to a network.

OTOH   (On The Other Hand) An abbreviation often used in online conversations.

packet   The unit of data transmission on the Internet. A packet that consists of the data being transferred with additional overhead information, such as the transmitting and receiving of addresses.

packet switching   The communications technology that the Internet is based on, where data being sent between computers is transmitted in packets.

parallel   Means of communication in which digital data is sent multiple bits at a time, with each simultaneous bit being sent over a separate line.

PDIAL   A list of mailing lists maintained by Stephanie da Silva (arielle@taronga.com), periodically posted to the news.answers, news.announce.newusers, and news.lists UseNet newsgroups.

PDN   (Public Data Network) A service such as Sprintnet that gives access to a nationwide data network through a local phone call.

peer-to-peer   Internet services that can be offered and accessed by anyone, without requiring a special server.

PEM   (Privacy Enhanced Mail) A standard for automatically encrypting and decrypting mail messages to provide more secure message transmission.

ping A utility that sends out a packet to an Internet host and waits for a response (used to check if a host is up) and estimates how much time it takes for information to pass back and forth.

POP (Point of Presence) Indicates availability of a local access number to a public data network.

port (hardware) A physical channel on a computer that allows you to communicate with other devices (printers, modems, disk drives, and so on).

port (network) An address to which incoming data packets are sent. Special ports can be assigned to send the data directly to a server (FTP, Gopher, WWW, telnet, e-mail) or other specific program.

post Send a message to a UseNet newsgroup.

postmaster An address to which you can send questions about a site (asking if a user has an account there or if they sell a particular product, for example).

Prodigy A commercial online service that gives its subscribers access to the Internet in addition to its other features.

protocol Standards that define how computers on a network communicate with one another.

provider Someone who sells—or gives away, in some cases—access to the Internet.

public domain software Software that is made available by the author to anyone who wants it. (In this case, the author gives up all rights to the software.)

RAS (Remote Access Service) A service that allows other computers to remotely connect to a Microsoft NT computer.

remote Pertaining to a host on the network other than the computer you now are using.

remote host A host on the network other than the computer you currently are using.

repeater Device that allows you to extend the length of your network by amplifying and repeating the information it receives.

RFC (Request For Comments) A document submitted to the Internet governing board to propose Internet standards or to document information about the Internet.

rlogin   A UNIX command that allows you to log in to a remote computer.

router   Equipment that receives an Internet packet and sends it to the next machine in the destination path.

serial   Means of communication in which digital data is sent one bit at a time over a single physical line.

server   Provider of a service. Also often refers to a piece of hardware or software that provides access to information requested from it. See also client.

server-side include   An SSI is a command that directs the server to run a program, usually in the PERL programming language. SSIs are server-specific.

SGML   (Standard General Markup Language) A powerful markup language that allows you to structure documents so that they can be displayed on any type of computer. The current HTML standard is defined using SGML.

shareware   Software that is made available by the author to anyone who wants it, with a request to send the author a nominal fee if the software is used on a regular basis.

signature   A personal sign-off used in e-mail and newsgroup posts, often contained in a file and automatically appended to the mail or post. Often contains organization affiliation and pertinent personal information.

site   A group of computers under a single administrative control.

SmartList   Software that automates the management of electronic mailing lists. See also listproc, LISTSERV, majordomo.

SMDS   (Switched Multimegabit Data Service) A type of high-speed digital communications protocol.

smiley face   An ASCII drawing such as :-) (look at it sideways) used to help indicate emotion in a message. Also called emoticon.

SMTP   (Simple Mail Transport Protocol) The accepted communications protocol standard for exchange of e-mail between Internet hosts.

SNMP   (Simple Network Management Protocol) A communications protocol used to control and monitor devices on a network.

SONET   (Synchronous Optical Network) A high-speed fiber optics network.

store and forward   A type of system that collects information (like e-mail) for a user, then forwards the information when the user connects to the system.

subscribe   Become a member of a mailing list or newsgroup; also refers to obtaining Internet provider services.

surfing   Jumping from host to host on the Internet, to get an idea of what can be found. Also used to refer to briefly examining a number of different UseNet newsgroups.

syntax   A statement that contains programming code.

T1   Communication lines operating at 1.544M per second.

T3   Communication lines operating at 45M per second.

tag   A reference for commands that are part of HTML. See also HTML.

TAR   (Tape Archive program) A UNIX-based program that creates packages of directory structures.

TCP   (Transmission Control Protocol) The network protocol used by hosts on the Internet.

telnet   A program that allows remote login to another computer.

terminal emulation   Running an application that lets you use your computer to interface with a command-line account on a remote computer, as if you were connected to the computer with a terminal.

thread   All messages in a newsgroup or mailing list pertaining to a particular topic.

toggle   To alternate between two possible values.

traceroute   A utility that enables you to find out how many routers are between your host and another Internet host. See also hop-check.

traffic   The information flowing through a network.

twisted pair   A type of wiring where pairs of communication wires are twisted together to minimize interference. Compare to coaxial.

UNIX   An operating system used on many Internet hosts.

upload   Move a file from your local computer to a remote computer.

URL   (Uniform Resource Locator) Used to specify the location and name of a World Wide Web document. Can also specify other Internet services available from WWW browsers. For example, **http:// www.nsf.gov** or **gopher://gopher2.tc.umn.edu**.

UseNet   A collection of computer discussion groups that are read all over the world.

user name   The ID used to log in to a computer.

VRML   (Virtual Reality Modeling Language) A language that lets you display 3-D objects in Web documents.

WAIS   (Wide Area Information Servers) A system for searching and retrieving documents from participating sites.

WAN   (Wide Area Network) A network of computers that are geographically dispersed.

Web Chat   An application that allows you to carry on live conversations over the World Wide Web.

Web Crawler   A Web search tool.

WELL   (Whole Earth 'Lectric Link) One of the first Internet public access sites.

WHOIS   A service that lets you look up information about Internet hosts and users.

WWW, Web   (World Wide Web) A hypertext-based system that allows browsing of available Internet resources.

X-modem   A communication protocol that lets you transfer files over a serial line. See also Y-modem, Z-modem.

Y-modem   A communication protocol that lets you transfer files over a serial line. See also X-modem, Z-modem.

YAHOO!   A Web site that contains lists of many topics to be found on the Web and includes a search tool to find sites you are interested in.

Z-modem   A communication protocol that lets you transfer files over a serial line. See also X-modem, Y-modem.

INDEX

tags

Check out Que® Books on the World Wide Web
http://www.mcp.com/que

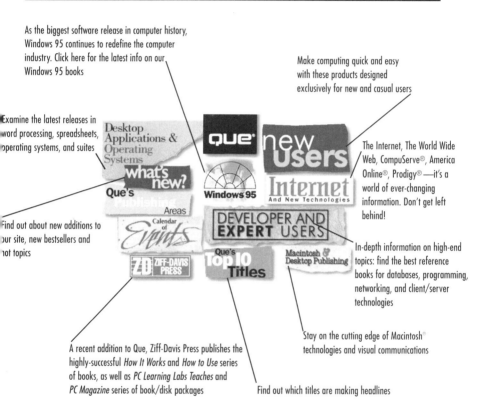

As the biggest software release in computer history, Windows 95 continues to redefine the computer industry. Click here for the latest info on our Windows 95 books

Make computing quick and easy with these products designed exclusively for new and casual users

Examine the latest releases in word processing, spreadsheets, operating systems, and suites

The Internet, The World Wide Web, CompuServe®, America Online®, Prodigy® —it's a world of ever-changing information. Don't get left behind!

Find out about new additions to our site, new bestsellers and hot topics

In-depth information on high-end topics: find the best reference books for databases, programming, networking, and client/server technologies

A recent addition to Que, Ziff-Davis Press publishes the highly-successful *How It Works* and *How to Use* series of books, as well as *PC Learning Labs Teaches* and *PC Magazine* series of book/disk packages

Stay on the cutting edge of Macintosh® technologies and visual communications

Find out which titles are making headlines

With 6 separate publishing groups, Que develops products for many specific market segments and areas of computer technology. Explore our Web Site and you'll find information on best-selling titles, newly published titles, upcoming products, authors, and much more.

- Stay informed on the latest industry trends and products available
- Visit our online bookstore for the latest information and editions
- Download software from Que's library of the best shareware and freeware

Complete and Return this Card
for a *FREE* Computer Book Catalog

Thank you for purchasing this book! You have purchased a
superior computer book written expressly for your needs. To
continue to provide the kind of up-to-date, pertinent coverage
you've come to expect from us, we need to hear from you.
Please take a minute to complete and return this self-addressed,
postage-paid form. In return, we'll send you a free catalog of all
our computer books on topics ranging from word processing to
programming and the internet.

Mr. ☐　　Mrs. ☐　　Ms. ☐　　Dr. ☐

Name (first) ☐☐☐☐☐☐☐☐☐☐ (M.I.) ☐ (last) ☐☐☐☐☐☐☐☐☐☐☐☐☐☐☐☐

Address ☐☐☐☐☐☐☐☐☐☐☐☐☐☐☐☐☐☐☐☐☐☐☐☐☐

☐☐☐☐☐☐☐☐☐☐☐☐☐☐☐☐☐☐☐☐☐☐☐☐☐

City ☐☐☐☐☐☐☐☐☐☐☐☐☐ State ☐☐ Zip ☐☐☐☐☐ ☐☐☐☐

Phone ☐☐☐ ☐☐☐ ☐☐☐☐ Fax ☐☐☐ ☐☐☐ ☐☐☐☐

Company Name ☐☐☐☐☐☐☐☐☐☐☐☐☐☐☐☐☐☐☐☐☐☐

E-mail address ☐☐☐☐☐☐☐☐☐☐☐☐☐☐☐☐☐☐☐☐☐☐☐☐☐☐

1. Please check at least (3) influencing factors for purchasing this book.

Front or back cover information on book .... ☐
Special approach to the content .... ☐
Completeness of content .... ☐
Author's reputation .... ☐
Publisher's reputation .... ☐
Book cover design or layout .... ☐
Index or table of contents of book .... ☐
Price of book .... ☐
Special effects, graphics, illustrations .... ☐
Other (Please specify): _____ ☐

2. How did you first learn about this book?

Internet Site .... ☐
Saw in Macmillan Computer
　　Publishing catalog .... ☐
Recommended by store personnel .... ☐
Saw the book on bookshelf at store .... ☐
Recommended by a friend .... ☐
Received advertisement in the mail .... ☐
Saw an advertisement in: _____ ☐
Read book review in: _____ ☐
Other (Please specify): _____ ☐

3. How many computer books have you purchased in the last six months?

This book only .... ☐　　3 to 5 books .... ☐
2 books .... ☐　　More than 5 .... ☐

4. Where did you purchase this book?

Bookstore .... ☐
Computer Store .... ☐
Consumer Electronics Store .... ☐
Department Store .... ☐
Office Club .... ☐
Warehouse Club .... ☐
Mail Order .... ☐
Direct from Publisher .... ☐
Internet site .... ☐
Other (Please specify): .... ☐

5. How long have you been using a computer?

Less than 6 months .. ☐　　6 months to a year ..... ☐
1 to 3 years .... ☐　　More than 3 years ...... ☐

6. What is your level of experience with personal computers and with the subject of this book?

	With PC's	With subject of book
New	☐	☐
Casual	☐	☐
Accomplished	☐	☐
Expert	☐	☐

Source Code — 0-7897-1144-3

7. Which of the following best describes your job title?

Administrative Assistant .... ☐
Coordinator .... ☐
Manager/Supervisor .... ☐
Director .... ☐
Vice President .... ☐
President/CEO/COO .... ☐
Lawyer/Doctor/Medical Professional .... ☐
Teacher/Educator/Trainer .... ☐
Engineer/Technician .... ☐
Consultant .... ☐
Not employed/Student/Retired .... ☐
Other (Please specify): .... ☐

8. Which of the following best describes the area of the company your job title falls under?

Accounting .... ☐
Engineering .... ☐
Manufacturing .... ☐
Marketing .... ☐
Operations .... ☐
Sales .... ☐
Other (Please specify): .... ☐

9. What is your age?

Under 20 .... ☐
21-29 .... ☐
30-39 .... ☐
40-49 .... ☐
50-59 .... ☐
60-over .... ☐

10. Are you:

Male .... ☐
Female .... ☐

11. Which computer publications do you read regularly? (Please list)

_____
_____
_____
_____
_____
_____
_____
_____
_____
_____

Comments: _____

_____

_____

Fold here and scotch-tape to ma

||"|"|"|"|"|""||"|"|"|"|"||"|""||"|"|

NO POSTAGE
NECESSARY
IF MAILED
IN THE
UNITED STATES

BUSINESS REPLY MAIL

FIRST-CLASS MAIL PERMIT NO. 9918 INDIANAPOLIS IN

POSTAGE WILL BE PAID BY THE ADDRESSEE

ATTN MARKETING
MACMILLAN COMPUTER PUBLISHING
MACMILLAN PUBLISHING USA
201 W 103RD ST
INDIANAPOLIS IN 46290-9042

MACMILLAN COMPUTER PUBLISHING USA

A VIACOM COMPANY

Technical Support:

If you need assistance with the information in this book or with a CD/Disk accompanying the book, please access the Knowledge Base on our Web site at **http://www.superlibrary.com/general/support**. Our most Frequently Asked Questions are answered there. If you do not find the answer to your questions on our Web site, you may contact Macmillan Technical Support **(317) 581-3833** or e-mail us at **support@mcp.com**.